Table of Conte

Chapter 1   Introduction to the Microsoft BI Stack

Chapter 2   Developing a Data Model with a SSAS Tabular Instance

Chapter 3   Learning DAX

Chapter 4   Preparing the Data Model for Reporting and Deployment

Chapter 5   Exploring the Data Model with Power View

Detailed Table of Contents

Dedication

I would like to dedicate this book to my wife for her unconditional love and support to inspire me to write this book. This book is also dedicated to my parents for their blessings. They have worked hard to make me capable enough to be what I am today. I would also like to take this opportunity to thank Microsoft for teaching me strong values and helping me realize my true potential. Last but not least, I would like to thank Syncfusion for giving me this opportunity to write a book to share my expertise on the product.

Chapter 1 Introduction to the Microsoft BI Stack

Before developing any business intelligence (BI) solution, it is important to understand the intention or the use case for the solution, what the end user or the analyst wants to derive using the solution, whether the solution will be used for dynamic ad hoc analytics or enterprise reporting, whether the end user prefers the report to be delivered to them (push), or whether they like to browse the report on demand (pull) and change the measures or dimensions based on their requirements (ad hoc).

The choice of analytics and reporting tool in our BI solution is dependent on this set of questions and other criteria. To ensure that we choose the best available tool that suits the requirements of the end users, it is important that we as BI developers understand all the tools available to us with their strengths and weaknesses. Sometimes a single tool may not fulfill all the requirements, in which case, we need to use a combination of tools.

In this chapter, I would like to introduce you to the Microsoft BI stack so that when we develop a BI solution for end users, we choose the right tool to best fit the user's requirements.

The rest of the book dives deep into developing SQL Server 2012 Analysis Services tabular data models for analytics and using Power View for data exploration and reporting, which are the new analytics and reporting tools introduced in the SQL Server 2012 Microsoft BI (MSBI) stack.

What is business intelligence?

Business intelligence is the process of converting data into information so that business decision makers or analysts can make informed decisions better and faster.

Although the term business intelligence is used more in the modern days of big data and analytics, the concept is not new to the world. The same concept was previously known as executive information systems (EIS) and later known as decision support systems (DSS).

The source of data can be anything ranging from flat files to a normalized online transaction processing (OLTP) database system, while the end products are reports that allow end users to derive meaningful information by slicing and dicing the facts.

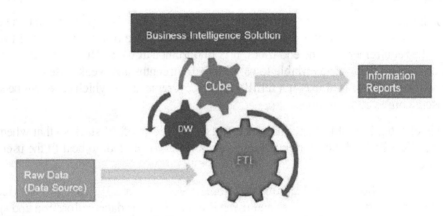

Figure 1: Business intelligence solution

Figure 1 depicts how a typical business intelligence solution looks sand what actions it performs. Let us briefly examine each component.

Extract-transform-load (ETL)

The raw data for the BI solution may be available from varied data sources, and it may not be available in a relational format. For example, some location data might be available from Excel worksheets, and some measures from applications may be in CSV or XML format which cannot be consumed as is.

The job of the ETL layer is to extract the data from varied data sources and transform it into normalized structured data that can be further loaded in a dimension model (the data warehouse).

If the source of the data is a structured OLTP system, the transformation required is minimal and is basically an extract and load operation.

With the introduction of new tools such as PowerPivot, Power Query, and SSAS tabular model, the raw data from data sources can be directly loaded in the cube without the need of ETL or even data warehouse layers.

Data warehouse (DW)

The data warehouse layer of the BI solution is typically an RDBMS database (things have changed with the introduction of big data and NoSQL), which is designed using dimension modeling techniques (the Ralph Kimball approach or Bill Inmon approach).

In the DW layer, data is classified as dimensions or facts based on its characteristics. A dimension gives the context to slice the data, while facts are measures of interest.

The dimension modeling techniques and detailed discussion on dimensions and facts are outside the scope of this book.

In the traditional data warehousing methods with multidimensional cubes, it was important to have a well-designed data warehouse using dimension modeling techniques. With the introduction of PowerPivot and tabular cubes, data no longer needs to be classified as dimensions and facts, which makes data modeling much easier in tabular cubes compared to traditional cubes.

Nevertheless, it is still recommended to have a data warehouse database designed to store data in a form suitable for reporting, aggregation, and cube processing.

Cube

The information available from BI solutions should allow end users to dynamically slice and dice measures (or facts) across different dimensions and further at different levels of the dimension hierarchy.

The DW stores the dimensions and fact data, which allows us to fetch static reports directly from the DW itself. However, the DW may not be able to handle the flexibility of dynamically slicing and dicing by different dimensions or various levels of the dimension hierarchy.

Thus we have cubes, which virtually store the aggregated data for each measure, level of dimension hierarchy, and dimension.

The cubes are data models which virtually appear to store pre-aggregated measures data across different levels of the dimension hierarchy, thereby giving end users the flexibility to dynamically slice and dice the measures at different levels.

The cube may not be required in a BI solution if the solution requires only static canned reports that are consumed by end users directly without any need for dynamic ad hoc reporting.

Reporting

The final layer of the BI solution is the reporting layer where users derive meaningful information from reported data.

The reports might be in the form of dashboard reports that display highly summarized data for executive users along with key performance indicators (KPIs) and visual indicators, or detailed reports that display each transaction that occurred as required by information workers.

The reports can also be classified as static reports, which are designed and developed by developers from the data warehouse, and are consumed by end users as is. Dynamic ad hoc reports, on the other hand, are exposed to end users via cubes, allowing them to dynamically slice and dice the data.

The reports might have to be delivered to end users via an email (push), or users might browse the report on demand (pull).

The reporting solution should be able to cater to all types of reports needed.

Understanding the Microsoft business intelligence stack

Now that we understand the basics of business intelligence, we next dive into the Microsoft BI stack to understand which products are available at various layers.

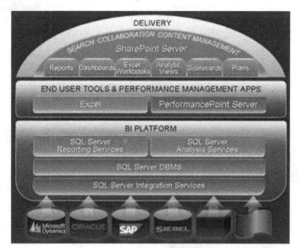

Figure 2: Microsoft BI stack

As shown in the previous figure, the Microsoft BI stack includes the following products:

SQL Server Integration Services (SSIS)

SSIS forms the ETL layer in the MSBI stack. SSIS packages accept data from various data sources like Excel, Oracle, SAP, and flat files, and inject the data into data flow streams where it undergoes various transformations available (union, merge, lookup, data flow, and execute SQL task, for example). The transformed data is loaded in the data warehouse hosted in the SQL Database Engine.

SQL Server DBMS

A SQL Server Database Engine instance forms the platform to host the data warehouse in the MSBI Stack.

SQL Server Analysis Services

SSAS forms the platform for hosting cubes in the MSBI stack. Until SQL Server 2008 R2, there was only one type of SSAS instance: a multidimensional SSAS cube. However, with the introduction of the new SQL Server 2012 xVelocity engine, we have new type of SSAS instance: the tabular data model. The tabular model is the primary focus of this book.

We will compare the traditional multi-dimensional SSAS with the tabular model, and look at how to choose the right SSAS instance later in this chapter.

Microsoft BI reporting platform

With the Microsoft BI stack, we have the following tools for reporting:

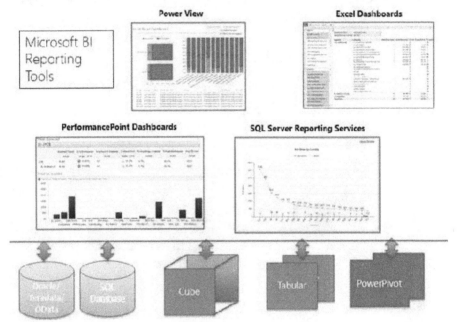

Figure 3: Reporting tools in the Microsoft BI stack

SQL Server Reporting Services (SSRS)

SSRS is a great tool for BI developers to build canned static reports for end users. SSRS is the most flexible reporting platform with vast set of visualizations such as gauges, indicators, and maps. SSRS allows reports to be exported to various formats including PDF, Excel, Word, and HTML. Further, the reports can be delivered by a subscription to file share, SharePoint list, or email.

PerformancePoint Services (PPS)

PPS is a great ad hoc dashboard and scorecard reporting tool for BI developers to build dynamic reports on SSAS cubes. PPS reports use SSAS cubes as data sources and allow end users to dynamically slice and dice measures across various dimensions defined in the cube. PPS reports expose the actions, perspectives, and more, defined in the cube.

Excel

Traditionally, Excel has provided the preferred reporting tools for most business users. Excel pivot tables and pivot charts can be used to explore the cube and perform ad hoc reporting.

Power View

Power View is the new Silverlight-based ad hoc reporting tool introduced in SQL Server 2012. The tool exposes the data model from PowerPivot, tabular models, and multidimensional cubes, thereby allowing users to dynamically handle the data. Power View provides a rich set of visualization tools that enhance the interactivity and experience for business users.

SharePoint BI dashboards

SharePoint 2010 and 2013 provide a platform to host all of the previously mentioned reporting tools on a single site, allowing developers to build rich dashboards. SharePoint is useful for team BI and enterprise BI solutions where all reports can be connected to build a single view dashboard for end users.

Later in this chapter we will compare all Microsoft BI reporting tools to choose the right ones based on our solution requirements.

What's new in the SQL Server 2012 business intelligence stack?

Microsoft made some heavy investments in the BI space with its SQL Server 2012 release, and some of the investments, such as the BI semantic model (BISM) and Power View, have put Microsoft in the leader's quadrant of BI and analytics platforms evaluated by Gartner.

BI semantic model

With the introduction of SQL Server 2012, Microsoft created the concept of the BI semantic model, or BISM. Many people have used this term interchangeably with the SSAS 2012 tabular model, which is not accurate. Let's try to understand what this new term means.

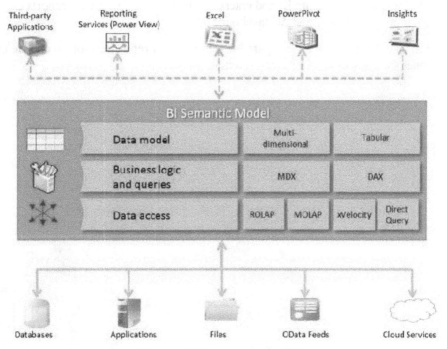

Figure 4: BI semantic model

As mentioned previously, with SQL Server 2012 we can now have two instances of SSAS: a traditional multidimensional model and a tabular model. From a developer perspective, designing and developing a cube in a multidimensional instance is completely different from a tabular model, the latter one being relatively easier. There is no migration path available to migrate a multidimensional cube to a tabular cube and vice versa. Further, the query language designed for multidimensional cubes is Multidimensional Expressions (MDX), while the language for tabular model cubes is Data Analysis Expressions (DAX). The design and development strategies for each model are completely different. However, the cube models can consume the same set of data sources and process the data.

The key feature introduced in these cubes is that a multidimensional cube can support DAX queries (this was introduced very late with SQL Server 2012 SP1 CU4), and a tabular model cube can support MDX queries.

This flexibility allows all reporting tools discussed previously (Excel, SSRS, PPS, Power View) to query either type of cube transparently with similar reporting features. For example, using Excel pivot tables and charts which produce only MDX queries, we can query either cube model (multidimensional or tabular) to build the same report with the same functionality.

From the end user perspective, both models provide the same functionality transparently. Hence, this new concept of the BI semantic model represents a transparent data model layer in SQL Server 2012 for all the reporting tools.

Choosing the right Microsoft analytics tool

With the SQL Server 2012 release, we now have three analytical tools that can be used to design a data model for reporting in PowerPivot for Excel, PowerPivot for SharePoint, and SSAS.

The following figure released by the Microsoft product team best explains the use case for each analytical tool.

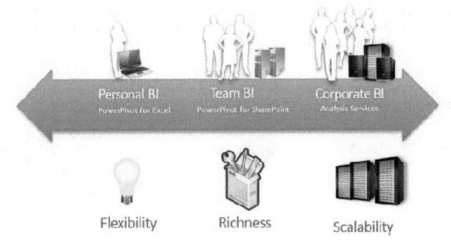

Figure 5: Uses and benefits of Microsoft analytics tools

Based on the target audience, a BI solution can be classified as personal BI, team BI, or corporate BI.

Personal BI

Personal BI is for individual business users or power users who like to create data models, KPIs, and measures for their own consumption and analysis. PowerPivot, which is now natively integrated with Excel 2013 and is available as an add-in with Excel 2010, caters to personal BI users.

Users can fetch data from various data sources (SQL Server, Oracle, flat files, OData feed, etc.) and load it in the PowerPivot data model in Excel. Further, they can define their measures, KPIs, and derived columns using DAX formulas within the PowerPivot data model and use them in the pivot table or pivot chart reports in Excel.

Team BI

Team BI is for groups of individuals who like to create, view, and share data models and reports. Over the years, SharePoint has evolved as the most preferred document library for organizations, and with the introduction of Office 365 (SharePoint Online), even small and medium businesses have adopted SharePoint as a document library. The Microsoft product team has designed and integrated PowerPivot with SharePoint so that PowerPivot workbooks uploaded in the SharePoint library can be viewed online using Excel Services. With SharePoint 2013, the Excel Services application natively loads the PowerPivot workbooks embedded within Excel.

PowerPivot for SharePoint serves well for team BI users due to its ability to provide scheduled data refreshes automatically, which is difficult to achieve with personal BI.

Corporate BI

Corporate BI is also referred to as enterprise BI or organizational BI. It's made for large groups of users with large volumes of data and varied requirements of data, security, KPIs, and measures. Data models defined in SQL Server Analysis Services specifically addresses the needs of corporate BI.

SSAS provides features such as calculated measures, KPIs, perspectives, role-based security, Kerberos-integrated security, and is capable of handling large volumes of data. A practical case study is Yahoo's data mart used for analytics and reporting. It is around 24 TB in size and is hosted on SSAS multidimensional cubes.

With the introduction of SSAS tabular model in SQL Server 2012, BI developers can choose between the traditional multidimensional approach and the new tabular model approach. In the next section we will compare these approaches to help you choose the right model for your BI solution.

Multidimensional approach versus tabular approach

Multidimensional approach

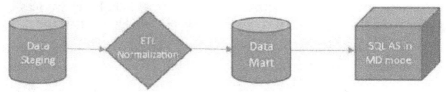

Figure 6: Process for multidimensional cube approach

Designing a multidimensional cube requires the data mart to be designed with a star or snowflake schema where the data is classified as dimension attributes or facts. The data from the dimension tables forms the attribute and attribute hierarchies in the cube, while the fact table forms the measure groups with individual measure columns forming the facts.

Since the data in the data mart needs to be in a star or snowflake schema, an SSIS package is required to extract data from various data sources, transform it, and load it in the data mart. The multidimensional approach requires an ETL solution to transform the data into a star schema in the data mart.

The multidimensional cube can handle role-playing dimensions, many-to-many dimensions, and parent/child dimensions out of the box, which gives us great flexibility in designing complex data models.

The multidimensional approach requires MDX knowledge for scripting and querying, which might be difficult for novices, but is one of the most flexible querying languages for experienced developers.

The multidimensional approach supports three different storage options: MOLAP, HOLAP, and ROLAP. MOLAP is the preferred option, as it provides the best performance at the expense of data redundancy.

From the resource (CPU, memory, or IO) and scalability perspective, the multidimensional cube consumes less memory than the tabular model and can scale well with partitioning and partition processing.

Tabular approach

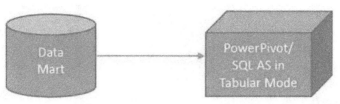

Figure 7: Process for tabular approach

The tabular approach uses relational modeling constructs such as tables and relationships for modeling data, and the xVelocity in-memory analytics engine for storing and calculating data. Unlike the multidimensional approach, the tabular approach doesn't require data to be organized in a star or snowflake schema, as it relies on compressed columnar storage of data. This makes data modeling pretty much easier with the tabular approach.

The tabular model may not be able to handle complex relationships (role playing dimensions, many-to-many-dimensions, parent/child dimensions) out of the box, which can make it less useful for complex data models.

The tabular model uses DAX for querying and defining calculations, which is relatively easier to learn and master compared to MDX.

The tabular model supports the in-memory xVelocity mode and DirectQuery mode (equivalent to ROLAP in the multidimensional approach). However, DirectQuery mode only supports data marts hosted on SQL Server. It currently does not support any other data sources.

From the resource consumption perspective, the in-memory mode for the tabular model is memory intensive with the amount of memory required proportional to the cardinality of the data, so it may not scale well in memory-limited environments. In some cases, the tabular model can perform better than the multidimensional model, depending on the data.

Decision matrix

The following figure outlines a decision matrix for developers choosing between the multidimensional approach and the tabular approach.

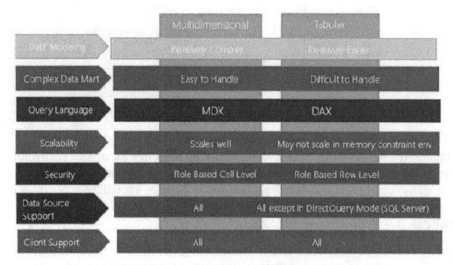

	Multidimensional	Tabular
Data Modeling	Relatively Complex	Relatively Easier
Complex Data Mart	Easy to Handle	Difficult to Handle
Query Language	MDX	DAX
Scalability	Scales well	May not scale in memory constraint env
Security	Role Based Cell Level	Role Based Row Level
Data Source Support	All	All except in DirectQuery Mode (SQL Server)
Client Support	All	All

Figure 8: Selecting a multidimensional or tabular model

Choosing the right Microsoft BI reporting tool

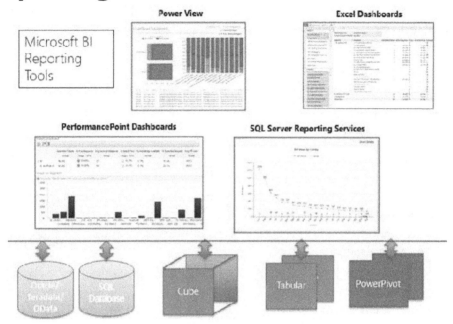

Figure 9: Reporting tools in the Microsoft BI stack

PerformancePoint Services scorecards and dashboards

- Interactivity: Scorecards and dashboards allow drill down and drill through capabilities, allowing users to perform ad-hoc reporting and analytics.
- Visualization: Compared to other tools, limited visualization and charts are available.
- Self-service BI: Users may not be able to develop dashboards by themselves.
- Export to Excel or other formats: Export to Excel is possible but other formats are not possible.
- Email subscriptions: Users may not be able to receive the report via email subscriptions out of the box.

Overall, PPS is a great tool for dashboards and analytics, but it doesn't support self-service BI.

SQL Server Reporting Services

- Interactivity: SSRS dashboards allow drill down and drill through, but don't support dynamic slicing and dicing. SSRS is primarily useful for static reports with limited interactivity and ad hoc capabilities.

- Visualization: Provides a rich set of visualizations including maps, gauges, sparklines, etc.
- Self-service BI: Users may not be able to develop dashboards by themselves.
- Export to Excel and other formats: Exporting to Excel and other formats such as PDF, Word, and HTML is possible.
- Email subscriptions: Users can create email subscriptions to have the reports delivered to their mailbox.

Overall, SSRS is a good reporting tool for static reports but may not be useful for ad hoc analytics and self-service BI.

Power View

- Interactivity: Power View dashboards allow dynamic slicing, which makes it a highly interactive tool for analytics and dashboarding. It is the preferred tool for ad hoc reporting.
- Visualization: Includes a rich set of visualizations, such as maps, scatter plot graphs, cards, tiles, etc.
- Self-service BI: Users should be able to develop dashboards by themselves.
- Export to Excel and other formats: Export to PowerPoint is possible but other formats are not supported.
- Email subscriptions: Users may not be able to create email subscriptions to have reports delivered to their inbox.

Overall, Power View is a good tool for self-service BI and ad hoc analytics wherein users can dynamically slice and dice information, but it doesn't support exporting data to a format other than PowerPoint.

Excel dashboards

- Interactivity: Excel dashboards in SharePoint via Excel Services provide limited interactivity with no drill-through action support. However, Excel workbooks downloaded from SharePoint support drill through.
- Visualization: Provides a limited set of visualizations, including tables and charts.
- Self-service BI: Users should be able to develop dashboards by themselves.
- Export to Excel and other formats: Export to Excel is possible.
- Email subscriptions: Users may not be able to create email subscriptions to have reports delivered to their inbox out of the box.

Overall, Excel dashboards are a good tool for self-service BI and analytics for Excel users, but have limited interactivity compared to other tools.

Decision matrix

The following figure outlines the decision matrix for developers choosing reporting tools for their BI solutions.

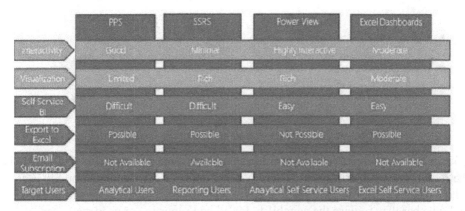

	PPS	SSRS	Power View	Excel Dashboards
Interactivity	Good	Minimal	Highly Interactive	Moderate
Visualization	Limited	Rich	Rich	Moderate
Self Service BI	Difficult	Difficult	Easy	Easy
Export to Excel	Possible	Possible	Not Possible	Possible
Email Subscription	Not Available	Available	Not Available	Not Available
Target Users	Analytical Users	Reporting Users	Analytical Self Service Users	Excel Self Service Users

Figure 10: Selecting the right reporting tool

Developing an MSBI solution

The following diagram outlines the steps involved in developing an MSBI solution:

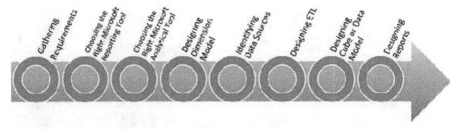

Figure 11: Procedure for developing an MSBI solution

Like in any software development lifecycle (SDLC), the first step of development is the requirement-gathering phase. Here we sort out from our customers or end users which measures they would like to analyze against which dimensions or attributes, and whether they require the capability for ad hoc reporting or need static reports created by the developer.

Once we have the requirements in place, the next step is to choose the Microsoft reporting tools that best suit the end user's needs based on the desired interactivity, visualization, self-service BI, export to Excel or other formats, and email delivery. For varied user requirements, we might want to choose a combination of reporting tools.

The next step is to choose the right Microsoft analytical tools (PowerPivot, PowerPivot on SharePoint, SSAS multidimensional or SSAS tabular). Depending upon the personal BI, team BI, or corporate BI requirements, we can choose the best analytical tool which suits the end user's needs. For a corporate BI solution, we can choose between SSAS multidimensional or tabular models based on the complexity of the data model, scalability, skill-set knowledge, client tools, and more.

The data warehouse is required for team BI or corporate BI scenarios. If the data warehouse is required (which is preferred), the next step is to design the data warehouse schema using the dimension modeling techniques given by Ralph Kimball. The data warehouse might contain multiple data marts with each data mart defined for a given business process. The data mart consists of a star schema with a central fact table surrounded by dimension tables with primary foreign key relationships. The fact table consists of key columns and measures to be analyzed, while the dimension table consists of the set of related attributes across which the measures need to be analyzed.

Once the data warehouse schema is ready, next we need to identify the data sources for the data warehouse, as the data warehouse will be populated from various data sources in the organization. Some of the data might reside in OLTP, and some might be available in flat files, while others might be available in the cloud.

Once the data sources for the warehouse are identified, the next step is to design an ETL solution to extract the data from varied data sources, transform them if required, and load them in the data warehouse. During this step, we might have to design an interim staging database where we first extract, load, and transform the data before loading it to the data warehouse.

After the ETL starts flowing, the data warehouse is populated with the data in a format suitable for reporting. For some reporting tools like SSRS, we can directly design reports to fetch the data from the data warehouse; however, if the user is looking for self-service BI and ad hoc reporting, a cube data model design is required. We can design the data model based on the analytical tool chosen earlier.

The final step in the development of a BI solution is designing reports as per the needs of the end user through the reporting tools identified previously, which will allow users to derive meaningful information and make informed decisions.

Summary

In this chapter, we covered the basics of business intelligence, the various tools available in the Microsoft BI stack, and how to choose the right tools for your BI solution.

In the next chapter, we start with data modeling using the SSAS tabular model introduced in SQL Server 2012, which will be the focus of the rest of the book.

Chapter 2 Developing a Data Model with a SSAS Tabular Instance

In this chapter, we will start with designing and developing a data model with the SSAS tabular instance using SQL Server Data Tools (SSDT, formerly called BI Development Studio).

As discussed in the previous chapter, unlike the multidimensional model approach, the tabular data model doesn't necessarily require data to be organized in dimensions or facts in the data warehouse. This makes tabular data modeling a preferred approach for relatively small data warehouse designs wherein the data might be available in disparate data sources, which can be directly loaded into the SSAS tabular data model for analytics. However, designing a data warehouse in a star or snowflake schema remains the recommended approach, since it stores the consolidated historical data, which decouples the data from the original (and potentially changing) data.

In this chapter we will use the AdventureWorksDW2012 database as our data source for the tabular data model. The AdventureWorksDW2012 database is a sample data warehouse database available from www.codeplex.com. The sample databases can be downloaded from this link.

Scenario

AdventureWorks is a virtual company that sells bikes, bike accessories, bike components, and clothing. The company sells its products through an online portal as well as through resellers. Each sales transaction via the Internet or a reseller is captured in an OLTP database (AdventureWorks2012), while AdventureWorksDW2012 is the corresponding data warehouse for this OLTP database where the data is organized in a star schema into dimension tables and fact tables.

The business analyst in the organization needs to analyze the reseller sales by geography; by product size, color, and weight; by its employees; and by date dimensions dynamically. For the given requirements, we have the following star schema designed in the AdventureWorksDW2012 data warehouse database.

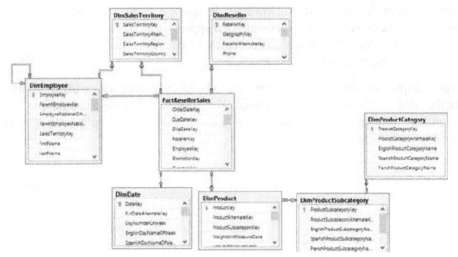

Figure 12: AdventureWorksDW2012 Schema

The requirement is to design a tabular data model for the reseller sales data mart so that business analysts can use Power View or Excel to dynamically sort the sales data to fetch reports for analytics.

Let's start by developing our Analysis Services tabular project in SSDT to understand the approach for data modeling.

Getting started with an Analysis Services tabular project

Similar to the multidimensional cube, SQL Server Data Tools (SSDT) is used to design and develop the SSAS tabular model cube. During the installation of SSAS, there is an option to select multidimensional mode or tabular mode when we reach the server configuration page for Analysis Services. A given instance of SQL Server can have Analysis Services in either multidimensional mode or tabular mode. However, if we need to install both modes of SSAS on the server, we will need to install two instances of SQL Server (run the setup again to install another instance).

On my development workstation, I installed a default instance of SQL Server that contains Database Engine, SSAS in multidimensional mode, SSRS, and shared components, and I installed a named instance of SQL Server (TABULAR) to install an SSAS tabular model.

After installation, when we start SSDT and click **New Project**, we will see the following templates available for business intelligence:

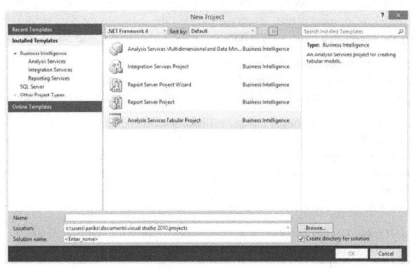

Figure 13: Business intelligence project templates

The **Analysis Services Tabular Project** is the new template available in SSDT.

In the **New Project** window, we name our project **AdventureWorks Reseller Sales** and click **OK** to create the project. The following window appears.

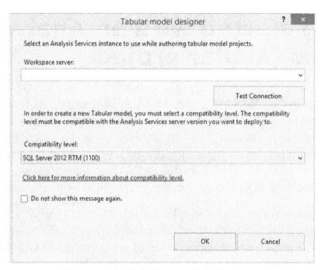

Figure 14: Tabular model designer

The **Tabular model designer** requires us to provide the SSAS tabular instance name, which will be used as a workspace server during the development of the project. During the development phase, when we process the data into the data model, it will actually be stored in a temporary database created in a workspace SSAS instance.

It is important to understand that a workspace server is not the instance where the tabular model cube will be deployed; the deployment instance will be separate and needs to be specified separately, which we will discuss further during deployment.

Whenever you create or open a tabular project, a workspace database is saved in the server's OLAP\Data directory. Over time, this folder may be bloated with temporary databases. From time to time you will need to get rid of the stuff in there you don't need anymore. To do that, you need file system access. Therefore, it is best if you pick a workspace database server that you can clean up. This is not required, but your server administrator will thank you.

In the first screen of the Tabular model designer, we provide our SSAS tabular instance name and click **Test Connection** to ensure we are able to connect to the workspace server. If the test connection fails, either the server name provided is incorrect, the server might not be reachable due to a firewall or other reasons, or the Windows credentials with which you logged in do not have permissions on the SSAS instance.

In this screen, we also have a **Compatibility Level** menu where we have two available values (at the time of writing this book):

- SQL Server 2012 RTM (1100)
- SQL Server 2012 SP1 (1103)

Each tabular model database is associated with a version of SQL Server it is compatible with and can be deployed to. If we are developing a tabular data model that will be deployed to an SQL Server 2012 SP1 instance, we should select the compatibility level as SQL Server 2012 SP1 (1103), and vice versa.

After specifying the workspace server and compatibility level details, click **OK**. The solution is created and an empty file called Model.bim is opened, as shown in the following figure.

Figure 15: New project

Import data to the tabular model

As discussed previously, the first step in designing a data model is to identify the data sources for the data. For the given requirements, we have all the required data available in the AdventureWorksDW2012 file.

In order to import the data from data sources, in SSDT, click the **Import from Data Sources** button, which is the first option in the toolbar at the top left corner as shown in the following figure.

Figure 16: Import from Data Sources button

When we click the **Import from Data Sources** button, the **Table Import Wizard** pops up and shows all the supported data sources.

Figure 17: Supported data sources for the tabular model

As shown in the previous figure, the tabular model project supports a wide range of data sources, including relational databases, SQL Azure, multidimensional cubes, flat files, and data feeds.

Select **Microsoft SQL Server** and click **Next**. In the next screen we provide the connection string for SQL Server by providing the server name and selecting

AdventureWorksDWDenali (which is our AdventureWorksDW2012 database) in the **Database name** drop-down. We provide a **Friendly connection name** as **AdventureworksDW** to easily identify the data source.

Before moving to the next screen, it is important to click **Test Connection** to ensure the connection to the database is successful and does not result in any errors.

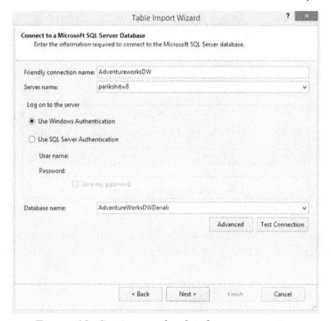

Figure 18: Setting up the database connection

Next, we need to provide Windows credentials which will be stored in the tabular model cube, and will be used to connect to the AdventureWorksDW2012 database to move data into the tables of the data model.

If the SSAS Service Account has permissions to read data from the data source, we can select the **Service Account** option, which does not require us to provide the credentials explicitly. This might be the preferred approach if the service account is a domain account and has permissions for the data source, which might be on a remote server.

Figure 19: Setting up Analysis Services credentials

The next screen allows us to import data directly by selecting the table or by writing a SQL query, which might be useful if we want to join multiple tables and import the data into a single table. Click **Select from the list of the table** to advance to the next step.

In this step, we select the individual tables that we would like to import and provide a user-friendly name, which will be the name for the imported table in the data model.

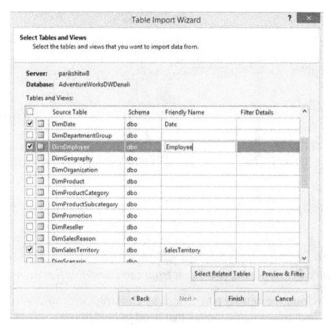

Figure 20: Selecting tables to import

For our data model, we select the following tables and provide the following names.

Source Table	Name
DimDate	Date
DimEmployee	Employee
DimSalesTerritory	SalesTerritory
FactResellerSales	ResellerSales

For the DimSalesTerritory, we filter out the SalesTerritoryAlternateKey column by clicking the **DimSalesTerritory** table and selecting the **Preview and Filter** option as shown in the following figure.

Figure 21: Filtering a column from the DimSalesTerritory table

In the same window, we can set row filters by clicking the drop-down next to each column header and selecting the boxes that need to be filtered.

In order to improve the processing time and save storage space, it is always recommended to filter out unrequired columns and rows.

In our scenario as well, we have a number of such columns that can be filtered out in each table, but to keep things simple, we will only filter out a column from DimSalesTerritory as shown in the following figure.

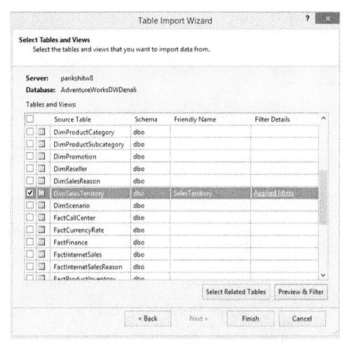

Figure 22: Filtered DimSalesTerritory source

Once we have all the required tables selected and necessary filters applied, we can click **Finish** to import the data into the tables in the data model. For a SQL Server data source, we also import relationships along with the data, which are visible in the last step, data preparation. For other data sources, we need to create relationships manually in the data model.

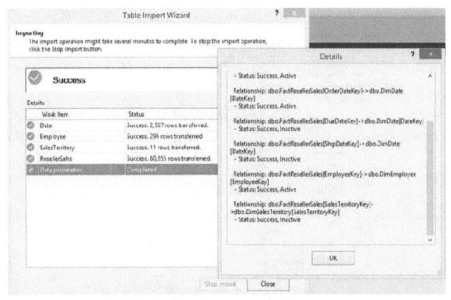

Figure 23: Importing data

Next we need to import the tables **DimProduct**, **DimProductSubCategory**, and **DimProductCategory**, but we do not need them to be imported as three separate tables. Instead, we would like to denormalize the three tables into a single table called columns.

To do this, we need to start the **Table Import Wizard** again and import the table by writing a SQL query that joins the three tables and imports the required columns.

Since we already have the connection to AdventureWorksDW2012 created, we can click the **Existing Connections** option on the toolbar to launch the Table Import Wizard as shown in the following figure.

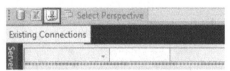

Figure 24: Existing Connections button

Figure 25: List of existing connections

Select **AdventureWorksDW**, and then click **Open**. The next window will give you options for how to import the data. Select the **Write a query that will specify the data to import** option.

Figure 26: Data import options

Next, we type the following TSQL query, which imports the data from multiple tables (DimProduct, DimProductCategory, and DimProductSubCategory).

```
SELECT
DimProduct.ProductKey
,DimProduct.EnglishProductName
,DimProduct.Color
,DimProduct.[Size]
,DimProduct.Weight
,DimProduct.LargePhoto
,DimProductCategory.EnglishProductCategoryName
,DimProductSubcategory.EnglishProductSubcategoryName
FROM
DimProductSubcategory
INNER JOIN DimProduct
ON DimProductSubcategory.ProductSubcategoryKey =
DimProduct.ProductSubcategoryKey
INNER JOIN DimProductCategory
ON DimProductSubcategory.ProductCategoryKey =
DimProductCategory.ProductCategoryKey
```

Figure 27: Typing a query to import data from multiple tables

Name the table **Product** and click **Finish** to import the data.

Note: For development purposes, while designing the Tabular Model in SSDT, it is recommended to import only a subset of the original database since all the data processing resides in a temporary workspace database on the workspace server instance.

We have now imported the following five tables from the data source into the tabular model:

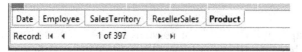

Figure 28: Imported tables

Modifying or deleting an imported table

If you are not happy with the table or columns that you imported from the table, you can delete a table or modify its columns. First, click the tab of the table you want to change at the bottom of the window. The following figure shows the Reseller Sales table being selected. Next, click the **Table** option in the menu. As the name suggests, the **Delete Table** option allows you to delete the table, while selecting **Table Properties** allows you to modify the table or the TSQL query used to import the table.

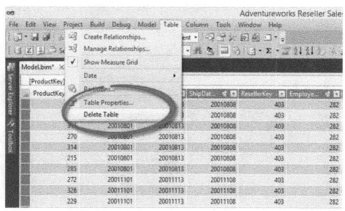

Figure 29: Deleting a table

Modifying or deleting a column in the table

We can either rename, filter, or delete a column after it is imported by selecting the column and right-clicking on it as shown in the following figure.

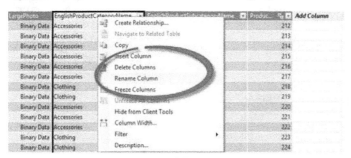

Figure 30: Modifying a column

In our data model, we imported all tables but we couldn't provide the column name (we can provide a column name in a SQL query by using a column alias, which we missed in the previous query). After the data is imported into tables, it is important to rename the columns to user-friendly names since the data model will be exposed to end users as is.

We will rename the following columns with new, user-friendly names:

Table	Source Column Name	User-Friendly Column Name
Product	EnglishProductCategoryName	Product Category
Product	EnglishProductSubCategoryName	Product SubCategory
Product	EnglishProductName	Product
SalesTerritory	SalesTerritoryRegion	Region
SalesTerritory	SalesTerritoryCountry	Country
SalesTerritory	SalesTerritoryGroup	Group
Date	EnglishMonthName	Month

Similarly, using the Table Import Wizard, we can import the data from various other data sources.

The following is a list of data sources supported by the tabular data model:

Source	Versions	File type	Providers
Access databases	Microsoft Access 2003, 2007, 2010	.accdb or .mdb	ACE 14 OLE DB provider

SQL Server relational databases	Microsoft SQL Server 2005, 2008, 2008 R2; SQL Server 2012, Microsoft SQL Azure Database 2	n/a	OLE DB Provider for SQL Server SQL Server Native Client OLE DB Provider SQL Server Native 10.0 Client OLE DB Provider .NET Framework Data Provider for SQL Client
SQL Server Parallel Data Warehouse (PDW) 3	2008 R2	n/a	OLE DB provider for SQL Server PDW
Oracle relational databases	Oracle 9i, 10g, 11g	n/a	Oracle OLE DB Provider .NET Framework Data Provider for Oracle Client .NET Framework Data Provider for SQL Server OraOLEDB MSDASQL
Teradata relational databases	Teradata V2R6, V12	n/a	TDOLEDB OLE DB provider .NET Data Provider for Teradata
Informix relational databases		n/a	Informix OLE DB Provider
IBM DB2 relational databases	8.1	n/a	DB2OLEDB
Sybase relational databases		n/a	Sybase OLE DB Provider
Other relational databases	n/a	n/a	OLE DB provider or ODBC driver
Text files	n/a	.txt, .tab, .csv	ACE 14 OLE DB provider for Microsoft Access
Microsoft Excel files	Excel 97–2003, 2007, 2010	.xlsx, xlsm, .xlsb, .xltx, .xltm	ACE 14 OLE DB provider

			ASOLEDB 10.5 (used only with PowerPivot workbooks that are published to SharePoint farms that have PowerPivot for SharePoint installed)
PowerPivot workbook	Microsoft SQL Server 2008 R2 Analysis Services	xlsx, xlsm, .xlsb, .xltx, .xltm	
Analysis Services cube	Microsoft SQL Server 2005, 2008, 2008 R2 Analysis Services	n/a	ASOLEDB 10
Data feeds (used to import data from Reporting Services reports, Atom service documents, Microsoft Azure Marketplace DataMarket, and single data feed)	Atom 1.0 format Any database or document that is exposed as a Windows Communication Foundation (WCF) Data Service (formerly ADO.NET Data Services).	.atomsvc for a service document that defines one or more feeds .atom for an Atom web feed document	Microsoft Data Feed Provider for PowerPivot .NET Framework data feed data provider for PowerPivot
Office Database Connection files		.odc	

In this section we imported the data from data sources into the data model. In the following section we will design the hierarchies, relationships, and KPIs to enhance the model for reporting.

Defining relationships

Once all the required data is imported in the data model and after applying the relevant filters, we should next define relationships between the tables.

Unlike RDBMS, which uses relationships to define constraints (either primary key or foreign key), we will define relationships in the tabular data model to use them in DAX formulas while defining calculated columns and measures. There are DAX formulas such as USERELATIONSHIP, RELATED, and RELATEDTABLE used in defining calculations that are purely dependent on relationships.

While importing the data from the SQL server data source, when we select multiple tables from the SQL database, the Table Import Wizard automatically detects the relationships defined in the database and imports them along with data in the data preparation phase. For other data sources, we need to manually create relationships after data has been imported.

In our case, since we imported the Product table by running the Table Import Wizard again, the relationship for the Product table is not automatically imported. We need to manually create the relationship.

There are two ways to create relationships.

In the first way, we click on the **Reseller Sales** table which has the foreign key ProductKey column, click the **Table** tab, and select **Create Relationships** as shown in the following figure.

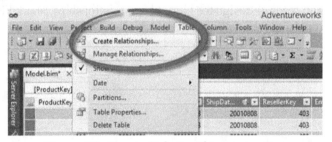

Figure 31: Create Relationships menu item

This opens the Create Relationship window. We can provide the **Related Lookup Table** and **Related Lookup Column** as shown in the following figure.

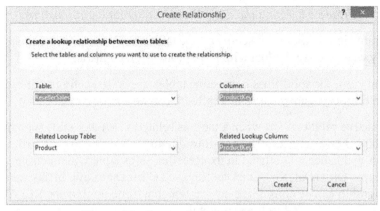

Figure 32: Create Relationship window

We can also define relationships using the diagram view. We can switch to diagram view by clicking the **Diagram** option at the lower-right corner of the project, as shown in the following figure.

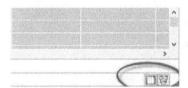

Figure 33: Diagram view option

In the diagram view, we can drag the **ProductKey** column from the **ResellerSales** table to the **ProductKey** column in the **Product** table and the relationship will be created as shown in the following figure.

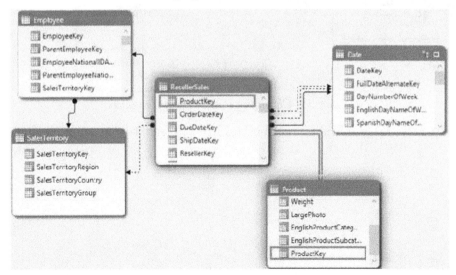

Figure 34: Using the diagram view to create relationships

The diagram view is useful for seeing all the tables and their relationships, especially when we are dealing with large, complex data marts.

In diagram view, the solid lines connecting tables are called active relationships, and the dotted lines connecting tables are called inactive relationships.

We see inactive relationships when a table is related to another table with multiple relationships. For example, in the previous diagram, the Date table is a role-playing dimension, and hence it is related to the Reseller Sales table with multiple relationships (OrderDateKey, DueDateKey, and CloseDateKey). In this case, only one relationship can be considered active, which will be used by the RELATED and RELATEDTABLE DAX functions, while the other two relationships are considered inactive and can be used with the UseRelationship DAX function.

We can switch an inactive relationship to active by right-clicking on the dotted inactive relationship and selecting **Mark as Active**, as shown in the following figure.

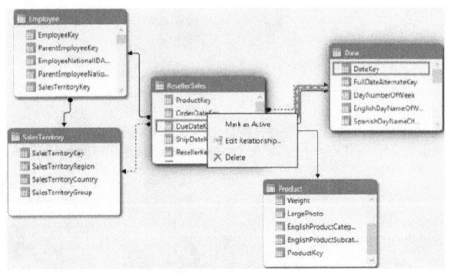

Figure 35: Changing a relationship to active

Now that we have defined the relationships, we will learn how to define hierarchies.

Defining hierarchies

Hierarchies are very useful for analytics as users navigate from high-level aggregated data to detailed data. Hence, it is important that the cube or data model supports the creation of hierarchies to allow users to drill down or roll up the data. Most dimension tables contain hierarchical data.

For example, the time dimension can have the hierarchy: Year > Semester > Quarter > Monthly > Weekly > Day. The Geography dimension can have the hierarchy Country > State > City.

The characteristics of a hierarchy are:

- It contains multiple levels starting from the parent level to the child level.
- Each parent can have multiple children, but a child can belong to only one parent.

In our data model, we can have following hierarchies:

Table	Hierarchy
Product	Product Category > Product SubCategory > Product
Date	Calendar Year > Calendar Semester > Calendar Quarter
Date	Fiscal Year > Fiscal Semester > Fiscal Quarter
SalesTerritory	Group > Country > Region

In order to create hierarchies, we need to switch to the diagram view. At the header of each table in the diagram view, we see an option to create a hierarchy.

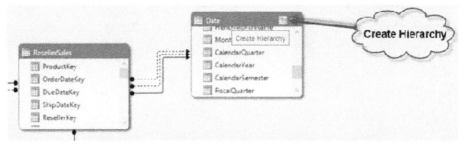

Figure 36: Create Hierarchy button in diagram view

When we click **Create Hierarchy**, it will create a new hierarchy object, which we name **Calendar Hierarchy**, as shown in the following figure.

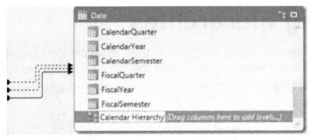

Figure 37: Creating a new hierarchy

Next, we drag the **CalendarYear** column from the table to the **Calendar Hierarchy**, followed by **CalendarSemester** and **CalendarQuarter** to form the Calendar Hierarchy as shown in the following figure.

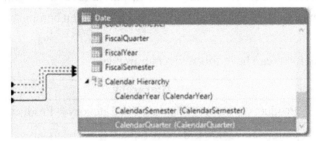

Figure 38: Creating the Calendar Hierarchy

Similarly, we create Fiscal, Products, and Geography hierarchies.

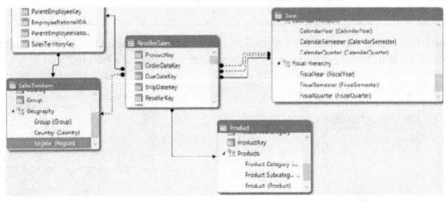

Figure 39: Fiscal, Geography, and Product hierarchies

Defining calculated columns

Calculated columns are nothing but derived columns defined using DAX formulas. Calculated columns are evaluated in row context, or in other words, for each row of the table.

In our data model, we have the Employee table in which FirstName, MiddleName, and LastName for each employee is captured in a separate column. However, for reporting and analytics, it would make sense to represent employees with their full name (FirstName + MiddleName + LastName). To do this, we define a calculated column called Name in the Employee Table to concatenate FirstName, MiddleName, and LastName of each employee.

To add a calculated column, we go to the Employee table and scroll right until we reach the last column. In the column after the last column we can start typing our DAX formula to define a calculated column.

```
=Employee[FirstName] & " " & Employee[MiddleName] & " " &
Employee[LastName]
```

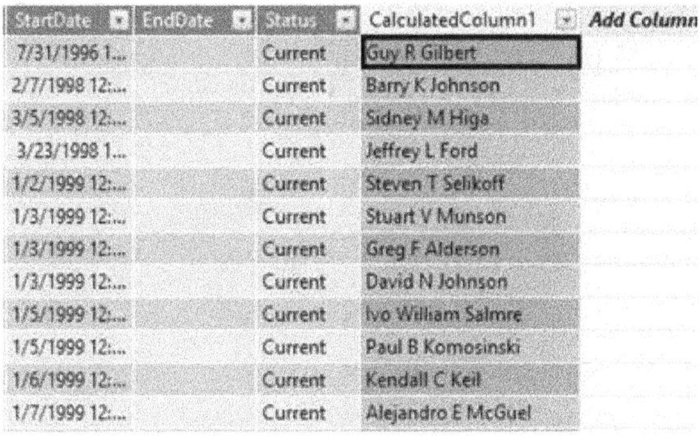

StartDate	EndDate	Status	CalculatedColumn1	Add Column
7/31/1996 1:...		Current	Guy R Gilbert	
2/7/1998 12:...		Current	Barry K Johnson	
3/5/1998 12:...		Current	Sidney M Higa	
3/23/1998 1:...		Current	Jeffrey L Ford	
1/2/1999 12:...		Current	Steven T Selikoff	
1/3/1999 12:...		Current	Stuart V Munson	
1/3/1999 12:...		Current	Greg F Alderson	
1/3/1999 12:...		Current	David N Johnson	
1/5/1999 12:...		Current	Ivo William Salmre	
1/5/1999 12:...		Current	Paul B Komosinski	
1/6/1999 12:...		Current	Kendall C Keil	
1/7/1999 12:...		Current	Alejandro E McGuel	

Figure 40: Adding a calculated column

By default, the column will be named CalculatedColumn1, which we need to rename as **Name** by right-clicking on the column as discussed previously.

In our data model, CalendarQuarter and FiscalQuarter are represented by numeric values 1, 2, 3, and 4; however, from a reporting perspective, quarters are represented as Q1, Q2, Q3, and Q4. Hence we define a calculated column using the following DAX formula:

```
="Q" & 'Date'[FiscalQuarter]
="Q" & 'Date'[CalendarQuarter]
```

Defining calculated measures

Calculated measures are measures of interest that are aggregated across various dimensions and levels of the dimension hierarchy.

In our data model, the ResellerSales table originates from a fact table that consists of the key columns used to look up the dimensions table and measure columns, which need to be aggregated. One of the key measures of interest in the Reseller Sales table is Sales Amount, which needs to be summed up across various dimensions. For this reason, we need to define a calculated measure called Sales to calculate the summation of Sales Amount.

Calculated measures need to be defined in the measure grid, which is visible in the section below the table tabs as shown in Figure 41. We define the calculated measure Sales using the following DAX formula.

```
Sales:=SUM(ResellerSales[SalesAmount])
```

 Note: Do not worry about the DAX syntax at this point. We will cover DAX in detail in the following chapter.

![Figure 41 table screenshot]

Figure 41: Defining a calculated measure in the measure grid

Next, we define the calculated measures Cost, Profit, and Margin using the following DAX formulas.

```
Cost:=SUM(ResellerSales[TotalProductCost])
Profit:=[Sales]-[Cost]
Margin:=([Profit]/[Cost])*100
```

Formatting the calculated measures to currency and percentage formats as displayed in the following figure is explained later in the book.

Figure 42: Measures with unit formatting

We will define more calculated measures as we learn DAX in the following chapter. In the next section we learn about defining KPIs.

Defining KPIs

Key performance indicators (KPIs) are the graphical and intuitive representation of the relationship between a measure and a goal.

As shown in the following figure, KPIs are status or trend indicators that can be used to highlight deviation of a measure from a goal.

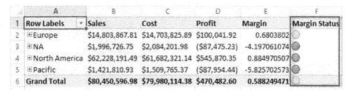

	A	B	C	D	E	F
1	Row Labels	Sales	Cost	Profit	Margin	Margin Status
2	⊞ Europe	$14,803,867.81	$14,703,825.89	$100,041.92	0.6803802	○
3	⊞ NA	$1,996,726.75	$2,084,201.98	($87,475.23)	-4.197061074	●
4	⊞ North America	$62,228,191.49	$61,682,321.14	$545,870.35	0.884970507	●
5	⊞ Pacific	$1,421,810.93	$1,509,765.37	($87,954.44)	-5.825702573	●
6	Grand Total	$80,450,596.98	$79,980,114.38	$470,482.60	0.588249471	○

Figure 43: KPIs

In our data model, we have defined the calculated measure Margin, which calculates the percentage profit over cost. Now, the organization wants to set up a KPI such that if the margin is more than 0.8 percent of the cost it is considered good, if the margin is between 0.4 and 0.8 percent, the profit is moderately good or average, and if the margin is less than 0.2 percent, it is considered poor.

To analyze the Margin, we define a KPI by selecting the cell where we have Margin defined, right-click it, and select **Create KPI** as shown in the following figure.

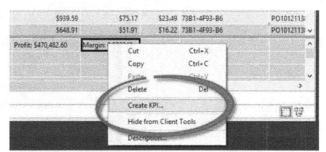

Figure 44: Create KPI option

In the KPI window, the Margin measure is already selected, and we can set the goal or target as an absolute value by clicking the **Absolute value** option and setting the value of the goal to "1" as shown in the following figure. We then select the status thresholds as 0.2 for the lower band and 0.8 for the upper band, and select the KPI icon style as the red, yellow, and green circular indicators.

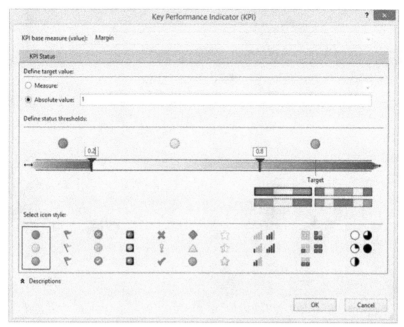

Figure 45: Setting up a KPI

Once we click **OK**, the KPI is created in the data model for the Margin measure. In order to verify the KPI we can browse the data model in Excel by clicking on the **Excel** icon in the top left toolbar of the project:

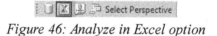

Figure 46: Analyze in Excel option

This opens an authentication window as shown in the following figure. We need to log in and open Excel using the **Current Windows User** option and click **OK**. The authentication and security is covered later in this book.

Figure 47: User options for analyzing the data model in Excel

Excel will open with a pivot table and a data connection to the model. In the **PivotTable Fields** window, we can drag the Geography hierarchy to the **Rows** area, and drag Sales, Cost, KPI Value, Margin, and KPI Status to the **Values** area as shown in the following figure. The resulting Excel report follows:

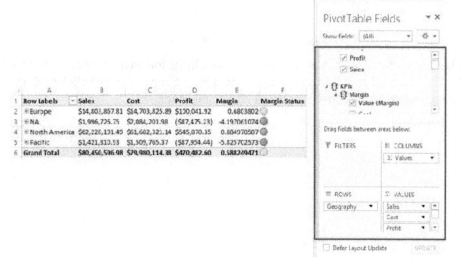

Figure 48: Data model analyzed in Excel

Filtering the data model

There are two ways to filter the row data:

- Filter the data while importing from a data source
- Filter the data after importing from a table

The first option is the preferred method; filtering the data while importing from a data source will help reduce the processing time and storage requirements. In the Importing data section, we discussed the various filter options. In this section, we will discuss filtering the data after it's loaded in the data model.

After the data is loaded, we can have the following filters depending on the data type of the column:

- Number filters
- Text filters
- Date filters

To filter the rows based on any of the columns, we need to click the drop-down arrow next to the column to see the filter options.

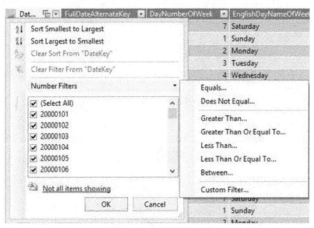

Figure 49: Number filter options

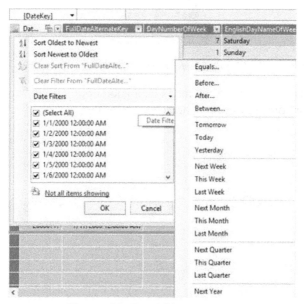

Figure 50: Date filter options

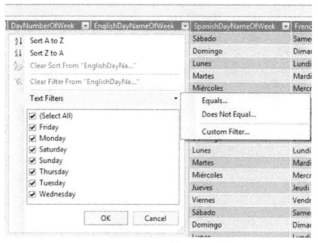

Figure 51: Text filter options

As shown in the previous figures, when we click the numeric column DateKey we see number filters, when we click the date column FullDateAlternateKey we see date filters, and when we click on the text column EnglishDayNameOfWeek we see text filters.

If we define a filter for any of the columns of the table, we see the following icon next to the column header:

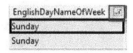

Figure 52: Filtered column header

Filtering the data in the data model might be a good option if we want to temporarily filter the data for some requirement and remove it later.

Sorting the data model

As shown in the previous figure, clicking the drop-down on a column header opens an option to sort the column in either ascending or descending order.

Depending on the data type of the column, the following options are available for sorting.

Data Type	Ascending Option	Descending Option
Number	Smallest to largest	Largest to smallest
Text	A to Z	Z to A
Date	Oldest to newest	Newest to oldest

Besides these sorting options, we have additional options to sort a column based on the values of another column. These are very useful and are in fact required in some scenarios.

In our data model, we have a Month column in the date table. The Month column is of text data type, and if we try to sort the month column by its own data values we will see the following report:

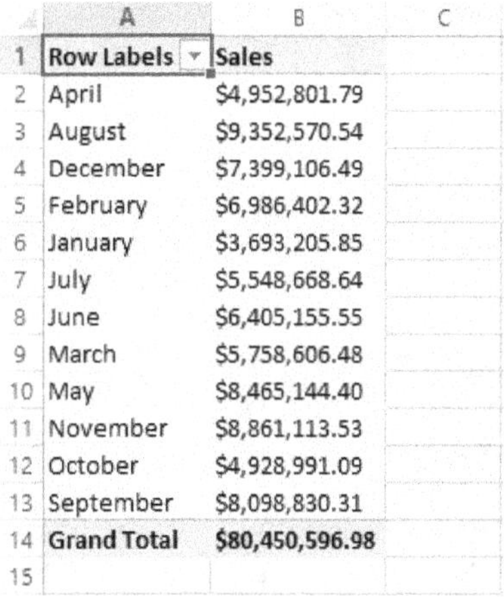

	A	B	C
1	Row Labels	Sales	
2	April	$4,952,801.79	
3	August	$9,352,570.54	
4	December	$7,399,106.49	
5	February	$6,986,402.32	
6	January	$3,693,205.85	
7	July	$5,548,668.64	
8	June	$6,405,155.55	
9	March	$5,758,606.48	
10	May	$8,465,144.40	
11	November	$8,861,113.53	
12	October	$4,928,991.09	
13	September	$8,098,830.31	
14	Grand Total	$80,450,596.98	
15			

Figure 53: Sorted Month column

In this report, the data is sorted by the Month values in ascending order with April at the top and September at the bottom, but this is not what we want. We would like the Month column to be sorted based on the order of months throughout the year instead of alphabetically. To do this, we will need to sort based on the MonthNumberOfYear column.

To do this, we use the **Sort by Column** option as shown in the following figure:

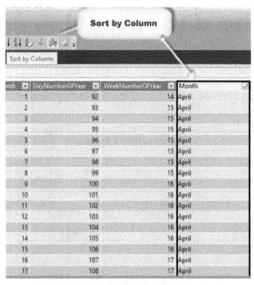

Figure 54: Sort by Column button

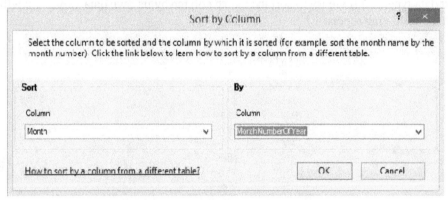

Figure 55: Sort by Column options

We select the **Month** column, click **Sort by Column**, and select
MonthNumberOfYear as the **By Column**. This will sort the Month column by
MonthNumberOfYear and will give us the report in the expected order.

Row Labels	Sales
January	$3,693,205.85
February	$6,986,402.32
March	$5,758,606.48
April	$4,952,801.79
May	$8,465,144.40
June	$6,405,155.55
July	$5,548,668.64
August	$9,352,570.54
September	$8,098,830.31
October	$4,928,991.09
November	$8,861,113.53
December	$7,399,106.49
Grand Total	$80,450,596.98

Figure 56: Month column sorted by MonthNumberOfYear column

Summary

In this chapter, we learned about developing a data model with SSAS tabular model using SSDT. In the next chapter, we will focus on the DAX language, which is used to define calculated columns and measures as well as query language for the tabular model.

Chapter 3 Learning DAX

Data Analysis Expressions (DAX) is the language used to define calculations in the tabular data model. DAX is also the query language used by the client reporting tools to query the tabular data model. In this chapter we will start with basics of DAX (syntax, operators, data types, and evaluation context) and later learn DAX functions.

A DAX query reference contains a number of functions that operate on the column of the table or table itself and evaluates to either a scalar constant or returns a table as well.

DAX syntax

When DAX is used to define calculated columns or measures, the formula always starts with an equal (=) sign. In DAX syntax, the column names of the tables are always referenced within square brackets [ ] and the column names are preceded by the name of the table.

For example, in the previous chapter, we defined the calculated "Name" column in the Employee table using the following formula:

```
=Employee[FirstName] & " " & Employee[MiddleName] & " " &
Employee[LastName]
```

We defined measures in the data model using the following formula:

```
Sales:=SUM(ResellerSales[SalesAmount])
```

In these examples, we see that a formula starts with an equal sign and all the columns are referenced as *<table-name>*[*<column-name>*].

When DAX is used as a query language to query the tabular data model, the syntax appears as:

```
DEFINE
    { MEASURE <table>[<col>] = <expression> }]
EVALUATE <Table Expression>
[ORDER BY {<expression> [{ASC | DESC}]} [, …]
    [START AT {<value>|<parameter>} [, …]] ]
```

DAX as a query language always starts with the EVALUATE keyword followed by an expression, which returns a table.

DAX operators

There are four different types of calculation operators supported by DAX: arithmetic, comparison, text concatenation, and logical.

Arithmetic Operators

Operator	Operation
+	Add
-	Subtract
*	Multiply
/	Divide
^	Exponentiation

Comparison Operators

Operator	Operation
=	Equal to
>	Greater than
<	Less than
>=	Greater than or equal to
<=	Less than or equal to
<>	Not equal to

Text Operators

Operator	Operation
&	Concatenation

Logical Operators

Operator	Operation
&&	Logical AND
||	Logical OR

DAX operators have the following order of precedence:

1. ^
2. – (Sign operator for negative values)
3. * /
4. ! (NOT Operator)
5. + -
6. &
7. <, >, >=, <=, =, <>

DAX data types

The following data types are supported. When you import data or use a value in a formula, even if the original data source contains a different data type, the data is converted to one of the following data types. Values that result from formulas also use these data types.

Data type in model	Data type in DAX	Description
Whole number	A 64-bit (eight bytes) integer value	Numbers that have no decimal places. Integers can be positive or negative numbers, but must be whole numbers between -9,223,372,036,854,775,808 (-2^63) and 9,223,372,036,854,775,807 (2^63-1).
Decimal number	A 64 bit (eight-bytes) real number	Real numbers are numbers that can have decimal places. Real numbers cover a wide range of values: Negative values from -1.79E +308 through -2.23E -308 Zero Positive values from 2.23E -308 through 1.79E + 308 However, the number of significant digits is limited to 15 decimal digits.
Boolean	Boolean	Either a True or False value.
Text	String	A Unicode character data string. Can be strings, numbers, or dates represented in a text format.
Date	Date/time	Dates and times in an accepted date-time representation. Valid dates are all dates after March 1, 1900.
Currency	Currency	Currency data type allows values between -922,337,203,685,477.5808 and 922,337,203,685,477.5807 with four decimal digits of fixed precision.
N/A	Blank	A blank is a data type in DAX that represents and replaces SQL nulls. You can create a blank by using the BLANK function, and test for blanks by using the logical function, ISBLANK.

In addition, DAX uses a table data type. This data type is used by DAX in many functions, such as aggregations and time intelligence calculations. Some functions require a reference to a table; other functions return a table that can then be used as input to other functions. In some functions that require a table as input, you can specify an expression that evaluates to a table. For some functions, a reference to a base table is required.

Evaluation context

DAX formulas or expressions are always evaluated in one of the following contexts:

- Row context
- Query context
- Filter context

Row context

When a DAX formula is evaluated in row context, the expression is evaluated for each row of the column referenced by the expression. Calculated column expressions are always evaluated in row context.

For example, in our data model we defined the calculated column using the following DAX formula.

```
=Employee[FirstName] & " " & Employee[MiddleName] & " " &
Employee[LastName]
```

This DAX formula is evaluated for each row of the Employee table, and hence is evaluated under the row context of the Employee table.

Query context

When a DAX formula is evaluated in the context of a query, the expression is evaluated by applying the filters defined for that query.

For example:

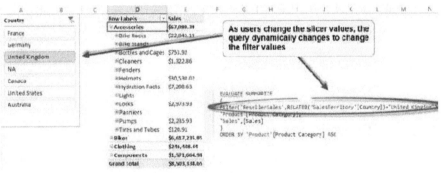

Figure 57: Dynamically changing query

In this Excel report, as the user clicks on various values of the Country slicer, the DAX query for the pivot table dynamically changes to reflect the filter value selected by the user. In other words, the DAX query is said to be evaluated in the query context.

Filter context

When a DAX formula is evaluated in filter context, the filters defined in the formula override any in the query context or row context. For example, in our data model, we define the following calculated measure:

```
FY04
Sales:=CALCULATE(SUM(ResellerSales[SalesAmount]),'Date'[FiscalYear]=2004)
```

This formula contains a filter for the fiscal year 2004, so it will always be evaluated under this filter context.

If the measure "FY04 Sales" is used in the Excel report with the slicer setting for fiscal year, the slicer selection does not affect the FY04 Sales measure value because the measure is evaluated in filter context, which overrides the query context.

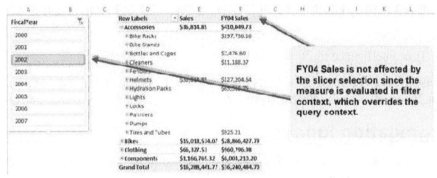

Figure 58: Filter context in Excel

DAX functions

The DAX language contains a rich set of functions, which makes it a powerful language for analytics and reporting. These functions are categorized into the following:

- Aggregation functions
- Date and time functions
- Filter functions
- Information functions
- Logical functions
- Mathematical and trigonometric functions
- Statistical functions
- Text functions
- Time intelligence functions

Discussing each function in the DAX query reference is beyond the scope of this book; however, we will discuss some commonly used functions from each category.

Aggregation functions

Aggregation functions are used for aggregating the columns. These are primarily useful in defining measures.

The following is a list of aggregation functions available in DAX along with a brief description of each.

Function	Use
AVERAGE	Returns the average (arithmetic mean) of all the numbers in a column.
AVERAGEA	Returns the average (arithmetic mean) of all the values in a column. Handles text and non-numeric values.
AVERAGEX	Averages a set of expressions evaluated over a table.
MAX	Returns the largest numeric value in a column.
MAXX	Returns the largest value from a set of expressions evaluated over a table.
MIN	Returns the smallest numeric value in a column.
MINX	Returns the smallest value from a set of expressions evaluated over a table.

SUM	Adds all the numbers in a column.
SUMX	Returns the sum of a set of expressions evaluated over a table.
COUNT	Counts the number of numeric values in a column.
COUNTA	Counts the number of values in a column that are not empty.
COUNTAX	Counts a set of expressions evaluated over a table.
COUNTBLANK	Counts the number of blank values in a column.
COUNTX	Counts the total number of rows in a table.
COUNTROWS	Counts the number of rows returned from a nested table function, such as the filter function.

Aggregation functions are pretty self-explanatory and simple to use. In the set of functions listed in the previous table, there are variations of the aggregation functions with an "X" suffix, for example, SUMX and AVERAGEX. These functions are used to aggregate an expression over a table or an expression that returns a table. For example, the syntax for the SUMX is:

```
SUMX(<table>, <expression>)
```

We can define a calculated measure as follows.

```
France
Sales:=SUMX(FILTER('ResellerSales',RELATED(SalesTerritory[Country])="France
```

In this formula, the FILTER function first filters the Reseller Sales for France, and later THE SUMX function aggregates the SalesAmount for the sales transactions in France.

The X suffix aggregate function gives us the flexibility to aggregate over a set of rows (or a table) returned from the expression.

Some of the aggregate functions listed in the previous table have an "A" suffix (AVERAGEA, COUNTA). The "A" suffix functions aggregate columns or data with non-numeric data types. All other aggregate functions can aggregate only numeric data types. For example:

```
COUNTA(<column>)
```

When the function does not find any rows to count, the function returns a blank. When there are rows, but none of them meet the specified criteria, then the function returns 0.

```
Regions:=COUNTA(SalesTerritory[Region])
```

The previous DAX formula counts the regions covered by the AdventureWorks Sales Territory, which can used in the following report.

	A	B	C	D
1	Row Labels ▾	Regions	FY04 Sales	Sales
2	Europe	3	$9,029,127.78	$14,803,867.81
3	NA	1	$1,251,447.21	$1,996,726.75
4	North America	6	$24,538,098.78	$62,228,191.49
5	Pacific	1	$1,421,810.93	$1,421,810.93
6	Grand Total	11	$36,240,484.70	$80,450,596.98

Figure 59: Using an aggregate formula for a non-numeric data type

Date and time functions

In a data warehouse or dimension model, date and time dimensions are conformed dimensions since they are used in all data marts for analyzing measures across dates and times. The Date dimension defined in the data model should have as many columns or attributes as possible (for example, Day, Month, DayOfWeek, MonthOfYear) to give end users the flexibility to identify trends in the data over time.

To support analysis across date and time dimensions, and to extract various attributes from Date columns, we have the following date and time functions.

Function	Use
DATE	Returns the specified date as a datetime.
DATEVALUE	Converts a text date value to a date in datetime format.
DAY	Returns the day of the month as a numeric value.
EDATE	Returns the date as a number of months before or after the start date.
EOMONTH	Returns the date of the last day of the month.
HOUR	Returns the hour as a numeric value from 0 to 23.
MINUTE	Returns the minute as a numeric value from 0 to 59.
MONTH	Returns the month as a numeric value from 1 to 12.
NOW	Returns the current date and time.
TIME	Converts hours, minutes, and seconds to a time value in a datetime format.
TIMEVALUE	Converts a text date value to a time in datetime format.
TODAY	Returns the current date.
	Returns the current day of the week as a numeric value between 1

WEEKDAY	(Sunday) and 7 (Saturday).
WEEKNUM	Returns the week number of the year.
YEAR	Returns the current year of a date, with integer values between 1900 and 9999.
YEARFRAC	Calculates the fraction of the year represented by the number of days between two dates.

The functions DAY, MONTH, and YEAR are used to extract the day, month, and year respectively from the date values. For example:

```
YEAR(<date>) , Day(<date>), Month(<date>)
=YEAR('Date'[FullDateAlternateKey])
```

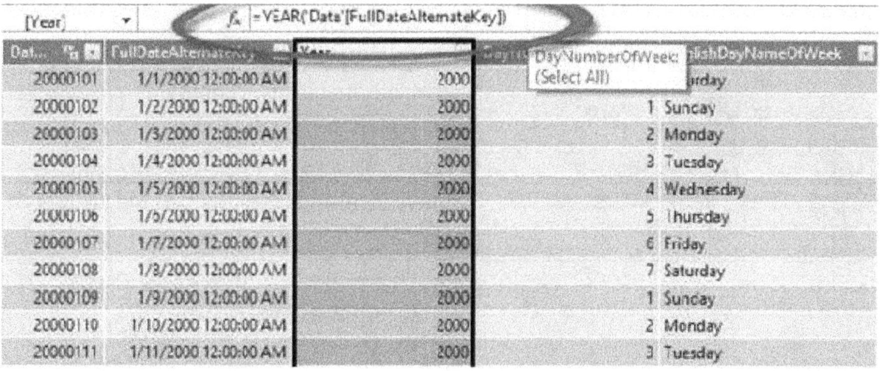

Figure 60: Using date and time functions

Filter functions

Filter functions are another commonly used set of functions, which we have already used in some prior examples. As we slice and dice the measures across the various columns of the table, we filter the data for those values of the columns, which is achieved by using filter functions.

The following table lists the available filter functions.

Function	Use
CALCULATE(<expression>,<filter1>, <filter2>…)	Evaluates an expression in a context that is modified by the specified filters in the function.
CALCULATETABLE(<expression>, <filter1>,<filter2>…)	Evaluates a table expression in a context that is modified by the specified filters in the function.

RELATED(<column>)	Returns a related value from another related table.
RELATEDTABLE(<TableName>)	Evaluates a table expression based on the filter context.
ALL({<table>|<column>[, <column>[, <column>[,...]]]})	Returns all the rows in a table, or all the values in a column, ignoring any filters that might have been applied.
ALLEXCEPT(<table>,<column>[, <column>[,...]])	Removes all context filters in the table except filters that have been applied to the specified columns.
ALLNOBLANKROW(<table>| <column>)	From the parent table of a relationship, returns all rows but the blank row, or all distinct values of a column but the blank row, disregarding context filters.
ALLSELECTED([<tablename>| <columnname>)	Gets the context that represents all rows and columns in the query while maintaining filter and row contexts.
DISTINCT(<column>)	Returns a table consisting of one column with distinct values from the column specified.
FILTER(<table>,<filter>)	Returns a table that represents a subset of another table or expression.
FILTERS(<columnName>)	Returns the values that are directly applied as filters to columnName.
HASONEFILTER(<columnName>)	Returns TRUE when the number of directly filtered values on columnName is one; otherwise returns FALSE.
HASONEVALUE(<columnName>)	Returns TRUE when the filtered context for columnName has one distinct value only; otherwise returns FALSE.
ISCROSSFILTERED(<columnName>)	Returns TRUE when columnName or another column in the same or related table is being filtered.
ISFILTERED(<columnName>)	Returns TRUE when columnName is being filtered; otherwise returns FALSE.
EARLIER(<column>,<number>)	Used for nested calculations where there is a need to use a certain value as an input and produce calculations based on that input.
	Returns the current value of the specified

EARLIEST(<column>)	column in an outer evaluation pass of the specified column.
VALUES(<column>)	Returns a one-column table containing the distinct values from the specified column.

Although the previous functions are categorized as filter functions, each is unique in the way it filters data. Let us discuss some of the filter functions here.

CALCULATE function

The CALCULATE function is one of the most commonly used functions used to evaluate an expression by applying various filters. Filters defined in the CALCULATE function override the query context in the client tools. For example:

```
CALCULATE ( <expression>, <filter1>, <filter2>… )
```

Previously, we defined a calculated measure as FY04 Sales, which uses the CALCULATE function to calculate the sales for the fiscal year 2004:

```
FY04
Sales:=CALCULATE (SUM (ResellerSales [SalesAmount] ), 'Date' [FiscalYear]=2004)
```

In the previous DAX formula, the sum of the SalesAmount is evaluated by filtering the Reseller Sales table for the fiscal year 2004. We see that the Fiscal Year column is defined in the Date table, but still it is possible to filter the Reseller Sales table using the fiscal year, due to the relationships defined between the tables. The CALCULATE function automatically uses the active relationship between the tables to filter the expression.

FILTER function

The FILTER function is commonly used to filter a table or expression based on the filter conditions. For example:

```
FILTER (<table>, <filter>)
```

In the previous example, to calculate FY04 Sales, we can calculate the same measure using the following DAX formula:

```
FY04
Sales:=SUMX (FILTER ('ResellerSales', RELATED ('Date' [FiscalYear])=2004), Resell
```

In this formula, we first filter the Reseller Sales table for the fiscal year 2004 and use SUMX to compute the sum of SalesAmount over the filtered Reseller Sales.

RELATED function

The RELATED function is another popular, commonly used function used in calculated columns or measures to perform a lookup to the related table and fetch the column values related by the underlying relationships. The RELATED function uses the underlying table relationships defined during data modeling to perform lookups on the related table.

The RELATED function requires a relationship to exist between the current table and the table with related information. The RELATED function allows users to lookup to the dimension or master tables similar to VLOOKUP for Excel. For example:

```
RELATED(<column>)
```

In this example, to calculate Total Sales for France, we used the RELATED function:

```
France
Sales:=SUMX(FILTER('ResellerSales',RELATED(SalesTerritory[Country])="France
```

In this formula, we filter the ResellerSales table using the Country column, which belongs to the SalesTerritory. Hence we use the RELATED function, which uses the relationship defined between the ResellerSales table and SalesTerritory table to filter the ResellerSales table for the country France.

ALL function

The ALL function is used to retrieve all values of a column or table ignoring any filters that might have been applied. This function is useful overriding filters and creating calculations on all the rows in a table. For example:

```
ALL( {<table> | <column>[, <column>[, <column>[,…]]]} )
```

In our data model, let us say we have a requirement to calculate the contribution of each country to the total sales. In order to create this measure, we define the following calculation:

```
Total Geography
Sales:=CALCULATE(SUM(ResellerSales[SalesAmount]),ALL(SalesTerritory[Country
% Geography Contribution:=[Sales]/[Total Geography Sales]
```

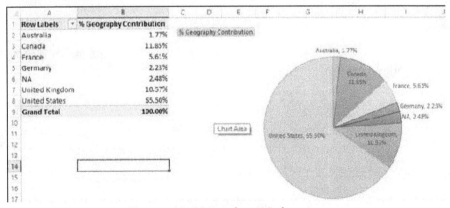

Figure 61: Using the ALL function

Information functions

Information functions are useful functions to check for the existence of some data value, blank, or error. Most information functions return Boolean values, so they are best used with an IF function.

Function	Use
CONTAINS	Returns TRUE if values exist or are contained in the specified column(s).
ISBLANK	Returns TRUE if a value is blank and FALSE if the value is not blank.
ISERROR	Returns TRUE if the value is an error and FALSE if not.
ISLOGICAL	Returns TRUE if the value is a logical or Boolean value.
ISNONTEXT	Returns TRUE if the specified value is not text.
ISNUMBER	Returns TRUE if the specified value is numeric.
ISTEXT	Returns TRUE if the specified value is text.
LOOKUPVALUE	Returns the value for the row that meets all criteria specified for search.
PATH	Returns a delimited text string with the identifiers of all the parents of the current identifier, starting with the oldest and continuing until current.
PATHCONTAINS	Returns TRUE if the item exists in the specified PATH.
PATHITEM	Returns the item at the specified position from an evaluation of a PATH function. Positions are evaluated from left to right.
PATHITEMREVERSE	Returns the item at the specified position from a string resulting from evaluation of a PATH function. Positions are counted backward from right to left.
PATHLENGTH	Returns the number of parents to the specified item in a given PATH result, including self.

CONTAINS function

The CONTAINS function returns a Boolean data type (True or False) depending on whether or not the value exists in the specified column. For example:

```
CONTAINS(<table>, <columnName>, <value>[, <columnName>, <value>]…)
```

Consider a scenario where the AdventureWorks management has decided to revise the sales target so that each country should try to meet the sales target of a 20 percent increase, except for the United States. Due to market conditions, management decided to set a target of a 10 percent increase for the United States.

To calculate the revised sales target, we use the CONTAINS function as follows:

```
Revised Sales
Target:=IF(CONTAINS(ResellerSales,SalesTerritory[Country],"United
States"),[Sales]+0.1*[Sales],[Sales]+0.2*[Sales])
```

	A	B	C	D
1	Country	Sales	% Geography Contribution	Revised Sales Target
2	Australia	$1,421,810.93	1.77%	$1,7...
3	Canada	$9,535,865.57	11.85%	$11,4...
4	France	$4,509,888.93	5.61%	$5,4...
5	Germany	$1,790,640.23	2.23%	$2,1...
6	NA	$1,996,726.75	2.48%	$2,396,072.10
7	United Kingdom	$8,503,338.65	10.57%	$10,204,006.38
8	United States	$52,692,325.92	65.50%	$57,961,558.51
9	Grand Total	$80,450,596.98	100.00%	$88,495,656.68

Figure 62: Using the CONTAINS function

ISBLANK function

The ISBLANK function checks the column value and returns a Boolean value depending on whether the column value is blank.

Blank is a special data type available in the tabular data model that is used to handle nulls. Blank doesn't mean 0 or a blank text string. Blank is a placeholder used when there is no value. Furthermore, in the tabular data model we do not have nulls, so when the data is imported the nulls are converted to blank values.

The ISBLANK function is useful for checking for blank values within a column. For example:

```
ISBLANK(<value>)
PreviousSales:=CALCULATE([Sales],PARALLELPERIOD('Date'[FullDateAlternateKey
YoY:=[Sales]-[PreviousSales]
YoY %:=IF(ISBLANK([Sales]),BLANK(),IF(ISBLANK([PreviousSales]),1,
[YoY]/[PreviousSales]))
```

	A	B	C	D	E
1	CalendarYear	Sales	PreviousSales	YoY	YoY %
2	⊞ 2001	$8,065,435.31		$8,065,435.31	100.00%
3	⊞ 2002	$24,144,429.65	$8,065,435.31	$16,078,994.35	199.36%
4	⊞ 2003	$32,202,669.43	$24,144,429.65	$8,058,239.77	33.38%
5	⊞ 2004	$16,038,062.60	$32,202,669.43	-$16,164,606.83	-50.20%
6	⊞ 2005		$16,038,062.60	-$16,038,062.60	
7	Grand Total	$80,450,596.98	$80,450,596.98	$0.00	0

Figure 63: Using the ISBLANK function in a data model

In this example, we use the ISBLANK function to test whether the current year's sales are blank, and if they are blank, a blank value is displayed. Further, if the current year's sales are not blank, we check to see if the previous year's sales are blank. If they are, we represent a 100-percent increase in sales; otherwise we calculate the percentage growth over the previous year's sales.

Similarly, we have the ISTEXT, ISNONTEXT, ISERROR, and ISLOGICAL functions which are used to test the value of the column and return Boolean values.

PATH functions

PATH functions are specifically designed to address parent–child dimensions. Unlike the multidimensional model, which automatically detects and creates a parent–child hierarchy, the tabular data model doesn't support the creation of a parent–child hierarchy out of the box.

In our data model, we have an employee table that has a parent–child relationship in which each row represents an employee who has a manager and the manager in turn is an employee in the same table.

First, we create a calculated column in the Employee table using the PATH function to determine the path of each employee to its parent.

```
=PATH(Employee[EmployeeKey],Employee[ParentEmployeeKey])
```

DepartmentName	StartDate	EndDate	Status	Name	Path
Production	7/31/1996 1...		Current	Guy R Gilbert	1 12 23 13 1
Production	2/7/1998 12:...		Current	Barry K Johnson	1 12 23 189 12
Production	5/5/1998 12:...		Current	Sidney M Higa	1 12 23 189 15
Production	3/23/1998 1...		Current	Jeffrey L Ford	1 12 23 189 17
Production	1/2/1999 12:...		Current	Steven T Selikoff	1 12 23 177 22
Production	1/3/1999 12:...		Current	Stuart V Munson	1 12 23 201 24
Production	1/3/1999 12:...		Current	Greg F Alderson	1 12 23 201 25
Production	1/3/1999 12:...		Current	David N Johnson	1 12 23 188 26
Production	1/5/1999 12:...		Current	Ivo William Saimre	1 12 23 111 28
Production	1/5/1999 12:...		Current	Paul B Komosinski	1 12 23 89 29
Production	1/6/1999 12:...		Current	Kendall C Keil	1 12 23 16 31
Production	1/7/1999 12:...		Current	Alejandro E McGuel	1 12 23 214 33
Production	1/8/1999 12:...		Current	Garrett R Young	1 12 23 188 34
Production	1/8/1999 12:...		Current	Jian Shuo Wang	1 12 23 138 35
Production	1/9/1999 12:...		Current	Simon D Rapier	1 12 23 9 39
Production	1/10/1999 1...		Current	Michael T Hines	1 12 23 186 41
Production	1/13/1999 1...		Current	Russell Hunter	1 12 23 76 45
Production	1/13/1999 1...		Current	Fred T Northup	1 12 23 214 47

Figure 64: Using the PATH function

As you can see, the column now contains the complete path of EmployeeKey from bottom to top stored as a single string value.

Now, for each level in the parent–child relationship we want to create a column. We use the DAX function PathItem for each calculated column to get the key of a specific level. To get the first level of the path, we use the following function.

```
=PathItem([Path],1,1)
```

To get the second level, we use the following function.

```
=PathItem([Path],2,1)
```

The output of the PathItem function will be EmployeeKey of the manager; however, we need the name of the manager, so we use the LOOKUPVALUE function to look it up as follows.

```
=LOOKUPVALUE(Employee[Name], Employee[EmployeeKey],PATHITEM([Path],1,1))
```

We define the calculated column for each level of the hierarchy using the previous LOOKUPVALUE function to form a flattened hierarchy as shown in the following figure.

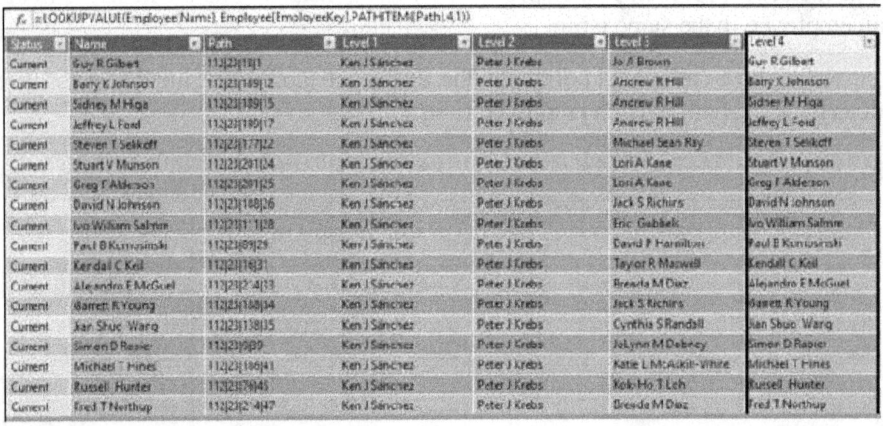
=LOOKUPVALUE(Employee[Name], Employee[EmployeeKey],PATHITEM([Path],4,1))

Status	Name	Path	Level 1	Level 2	Level 3	Level 4
Current	Guy R Gilbert	112|23|13|1	Ken J Sánchez	Peter J Krebs	Jo A Brown	Guy R Gilbert
Current	Barry K Johnson	112|23|149|12	Ken J Sánchez	Peter J Krebs	Andrew R Hill	Barry K Johnson
Current	Sidney M Higa	112|23|189|15	Ken J Sánchez	Peter J Krebs	Andrew R Hill	Sidney M Higa
Current	Jeffrey L Ford	112|23|190|17	Ken J Sánchez	Peter J Krebs	Andrew R Hill	Jeffrey L Ford
Current	Steven T Selikoff	112|23|177|22	Ken J Sánchez	Peter J Krebs	Michael Sean Ray	Steven T Selikoff
Current	Stuart V Munson	112|23|201|24	Ken J Sánchez	Peter J Krebs	Lori A Kane	Stuart V Munson
Current	Greg F Alderson	112|23|201|25	Ken J Sánchez	Peter J Krebs	Lori A Kane	Greg F Alderson
Current	David N Johnson	112|23|188|26	Ken J Sánchez	Peter J Krebs	Jack S Richins	David N Johnson
Current	Ivo William Salmre	112|23|171|28	Ken J Sánchez	Peter J Krebs	Eric Gubbels	Ivo William Salmre
Current	Paul B Komosinski	112|23|89|29	Ken J Sánchez	Peter J Krebs	David P Hamilton	Paul B Komosinski
Current	Kendall C Keil	112|23|16|31	Ken J Sánchez	Peter J Krebs	Taylor R Maxwell	Kendall C Keil
Current	Alejandro E McGuel	112|23|214|33	Ken J Sánchez	Peter J Krebs	Brenda M Diaz	Alejandro E McGuel
Current	Garrett R Young	112|23|188|34	Ken J Sánchez	Peter J Krebs	Jack S Richins	Garrett R Young
Current	Jian Shuo Wang	112|23|138|35	Ken J Sánchez	Peter J Krebs	Cynthia S Randall	Jian Shuo Wang
Current	Simon D Rapier	112|23|9|39	Ken J Sánchez	Peter J Krebs	JoLynn M Dobney	Simon D Rapier
Current	Michael T Hines	112|23|186|41	Ken J Sánchez	Peter J Krebs	Katie L McAskill-White	Michael T Hines
Current	Russell Hunter	112|23|79|45	Ken J Sánchez	Peter J Krebs	Kok-Ho T Loh	Russell Hunter
Current	Fred T Northup	112|23|214|47	Ken J Sánchez	Peter J Krebs	Brenda M Diaz	Fred T Northup

Figure 65: Using PathItem and LOOKUPVALUE to list hierarchy levels

Next, we create an Employees hierarchy by switching to the diagram view:

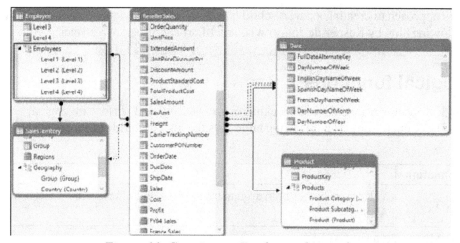

Figure 66: Creating an Employees hierarchy

Now, we browse the hierarchy in Excel:

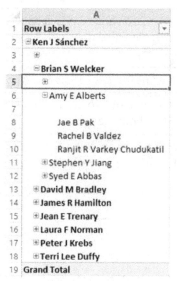

	A
1	**Row Labels** ▾
2	⊟ **Ken J Sánchez**
3	⊞
4	⊟ **Brian S Welcker**
5	⊞
6	⊟ Amy E Alberts
7	
8	Jae B Pak
9	Rachel B Valdez
10	Ranjit R Varkey Chudukatil
11	⊞ Stephen Y Jiang
12	⊞ Syed E Abbas
13	⊞ **David M Bradley**
14	⊞ **James R Hamilton**
15	⊞ **Jean E Trenary**
16	⊞ Laura F Norman
17	⊞ Peter J Krebs
18	⊞ **Terri Lee Duffy**
19	**Grand Total**

Figure 67: Employees hierarchy in Excel

The flaws with each approach for creating a parent–child hierarchy are:

- The number of levels in the parent-child hierarchy should be known in advance so that we can create the calculated column for each level.

- If we have a ragged hierarchy, some levels are blank—hence blank values in the hierarchy in Figure 67. However, we can handle blank values by using the ISBLANK function.

This approach to creating a parent–child hierarchy using Path functions references the following blog by Kasper de Jonge, who is a Microsoft program manager: http://www.powerpivotblog.nl/powerpivot-denali-parent-child-using-dax/

Logical functions

Logical functions are useful in checking, error handling, and performing logical AND/OR operations. The following table lists the logical functions supported by DAX.

Function	Use
AND	Evaluates whether both arguments are true and returns either TRUE or FALSE.
FALSE	Returns FALSE.
IF	Evaluates the first argument as a logical test and returns one value if the condition is TRUE and another value if the condition is FALSE.
IFERROR	Evaluates an expression and returns a specified value if the expression returns an error. If the value does not return an error, then the value is returned.
NOT	Changes the value of logical TRUE or FALSE.
OR	Evaluates whether one of two arguments is true and returns TRUE if one is true or FALSE if both are false.
SWITCH	Evaluates an expression against a list of values and returns one possible expression. This function is very similar to a SWITCH function in C++ or C#.
TRUE	Returns TRUE.

Most of the functions listed in this category are self-explanatory and commonly used in other programming languages.

IFERROR is a special function used for error handling in DAX, which we will discuss in more detail. IFERROR is actually a combination of two functions, IF and ISERROR. Since they are commonly used in tandem for error handling, the SSAS product team decided to have a dedicated IFERROR function. For example:

```
IFERROR(value, value_if_error)
```

In a previous example, to calculate year-over-year (YoY) percentages, we used the ISBLANK function to handle blank values from the previous year. However, we can also use the IFERROR function to achieve similar results, as shown in the following example.

```
YoY %:=IF(ISBLANK([Sales]),BLANK(),IFERROR([YoY]/[PreviousSales],BLANK()))
```

Mathematical functions

Since DAX is an analytical query language, it has to support mathematical functions useful for analytics and reporting. DAX supports the following mathematical functions.

Function	Use
ABS	Returns the absolute value of a numeric argument.
CEILING	Rounds a number up to the nearest integer value or significant multiple.
CURRENCY	Evaluates the value passed as an argument and returns the result as currency.
EXP	Returns the value of *e* (2.71828182845904) raised to the power specified.
FACT	Returns the factorial of a numeric value.
FLOOR	Rounds a number down to the nearest significant multiple.
INT	Rounds a numeric value down to the nearest integer value.
ISO.CEILING	Rounds a number up to the nearest integer value or significant multiple.
LN	Returns the natural logarithm of a numeric value.
LOG	Returns the logarithm of a number to the base you specify.
LOG10	Returns the base-10 logarithm of a number.
MROUND	Returns a number rounded to the desired multiple.
PI	Returns the value of Pi, 3.14159265358979, accurate to 15 digits.
POWER	Returns the result of a number raised to a power.
QUOTIENT	Performs division and returns only the integer portion of the division result.
RAND	Returns a random number greater than or equal to 0 and less than 1, evenly distributed.
RANDBETWEEN	Returns a random number in the range between two numbers you specify.
ROUND	Rounds a number to the specified number of digits.
ROUNDDOWN	Rounds a numeric value down.

ROUNDUP	Rounds a numeric value up.
SIGN	Determines the sign of a numeric value and returns 1 for positive, 0 for zero, or -1 for negative values.
SQRT	Returns the square root of a numeric value.
SUM	Returns the sum of all numbers in a column.
SUMX	Returns the sum of an expression evaluated for each row in a table.
TRUNC	Truncates a number to an integer by removing the decimal portion of the number.

I believe the functions are pretty self-explanatory and don't need detailed elaboration. If necessary, we can refer to online documentation for syntax of the functions and put them to use.

Statistical functions

DAX supports the following list of statistical functions. Note that there is some overlap between aggregate and statistical functions (SUMX, COUNT, AVERAGE, etc.).

Function	Use
ADDCOLUMNS	Adds calculated columns to a table or table expression.
AVERAGE	Returns the arithmetic mean of the numbers in a column.
AVERAGEA	Returns the arithmetic mean of the numbers in a column, but handles non-numeric values
AVERAGEX	Calculates the arithmetic mean of a set of expressions over a table.
COUNT	Counts the number of cells in a column that contain numbers.
COUNTA	Counts the number of cells in a column that are not empty, regardless of data type.
COUNTAX	Counts the number of rows in a table where the specified expression results in a nonblank value.
COUNTBLANK	Counts the number of blank cells in a column.
COUNTROWS	Counts the number of rows in the specified table or tabular expression.

COUNTX	Counts the number of rows that evaluate to a number.
CROSSJOIN	Returns a table that contains the Cartesian product of all rows from all tables in the arguments.
DISTINCTCOUNT	Counts the number of distinct cells in a column of numbers.
GENERATE	Returns a table with the Cartesian product between each row in table1 and the table that results from evaluating table2.
GENERATEALL	Returns a table with the Cartesian product between each row in table1 and the table that results from evaluating table2.
MAX	Returns the largest numeric value contained in a column.
MAXA	Returns the largest value in a column, including Boolean and blank values.
MAXX	Evaluates an expression for each row of a table and returns the largest numeric value.
MIN	Returns the smallest numeric value in a column.
MINA	Returns the smallest numeric value in a column including Boolean and blank values.
MINX	Returns the smallest numeric value after evaluating an expression for each row of a table.
RANK.EQ	Returns the ranking of a number in a list of numbers.
RANKX	Returns the ranking of a number in a list of numbers for each row in the table argument.
ROW	Returns a table consisting of a single row using expressions for each column.
SAMPLE	Returns a sample of rows from a specified table, with the number of rows determined by the user.
STDEV.P	Returns the population standard deviation.
STDEV.S	Returns the sample standard deviation.
STDEVX.P	Returns the population standard deviation.
STDEVX.S	Returns the sample standard deviation.
SUMMARIZE	Returns a summary table.
TOPN	Returns the top N rows of a table where N is a numeric value specified by the user.
VAR.P	Returns the variance for a sample population.

VAR.S	Returns the variance estimate for a population.
VARX.P	Returns the variance estimate for a population.
VARX.S	Returns the variance for a sample population.

Some of the statistical functions (such as GENERATE, SUMMARIZE, CROSSJOIN, and TOPN) are useful functions when we use DAX as a query language in client tools. In this section we will discuss RANK functions.

RANKX function

The RANKX function, as the name suggests, is used to rank a column based on an expression or measure. For example:

```
RANKX(<table>, <expression>[, <value>[, <order>[, <ties>]]])
```

Consider a scenario where AdventureWorks wishes to rank the products based on their demand and order quantities for the product. To achieve this, we first define a calculated measure, Orders, to capture the order quantity.

```
Orders:=SUM(ResellerSales[OrderQuantity])
```

Next we use the RANKX function in the Products table to define a calculated column, which ranks the products on the basis of the measure Orders.

```
=RANKX(Product, [Orders])
```

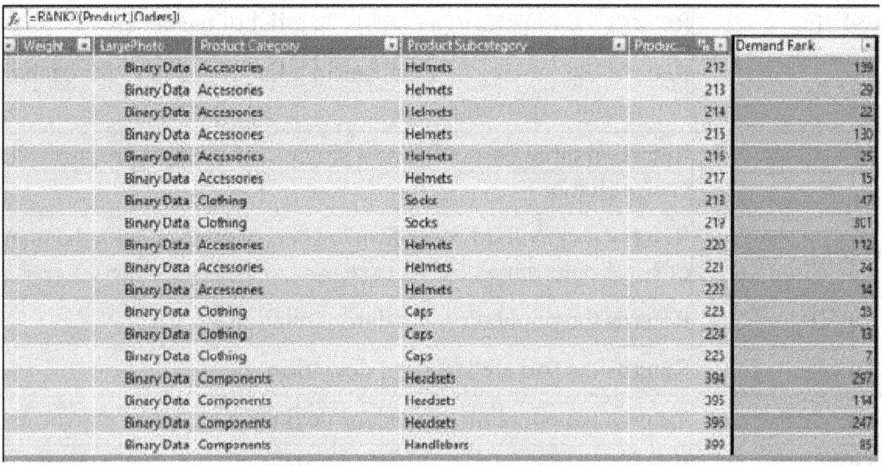

Figure 68: Using the RANKX function

Text functions

Text functions are similar to string manipulation functions. These are the text functions available in the DAX query reference:

Function	Use
REPLACE	Replaces part of a text string with different text.
REPT	Repeats the text the number of times specified in the parameter.
RIGHT	Returns the specified number of characters from the end of a string.
SEARCH	Returns the number of the character at which a specific character or text string is first found, reading left to right. Search is case-insensitive and accent sensitive.
SUBSTITUTE	Replaces existing text with new text.
TRIM	Removes leading and trailing spaces from a string.
UPPER	Converts a string to upper case.
VALUE	Converts a text representation of a numeric value to a number.
BLANK	Returns a BLANK value.
CONCATENATE	Concatenates two text strings.
EXACT	Compares two text strings and returns TRUE if they are exactly the same, including case.
FIND	Returns the starting position of one text string within another text string.
FIXED	Rounds a number to the specified number of decimals and returns the result as text.
FORMAT	Converts a value to text.
LEFT	Returns the specified number of characters from the start of a text string.
LEN	Returns the number of characters in a string of text.
LOWER	Converts a text string to lower case.
MID	Returns a string of characters based on a starting position and length.

Most text functions are self-explanatory and pretty straightforward, so we will not discuss them in detail. In fact we have already used FORMAT and CONCATENATE functions in some previous examples.

Time intelligence functions

As discussed previously, date and time are conformed dimensions in the data warehouse as most analysis is performed across the time axis, such as comparing measures like YoY, QoQ, and MoM, and calculating YTD, QTD, and MTD. Time intelligence functions are available to facilitate such calculations.

Function	Use
CLOSINGBALANCEMONTH CLOSINGBALANCEQUARTER CLOSINGBALANCEYEAR	Calculates a value at the calendar end of the given period.
OPENINGBALANCEMONTH OPENINGBALANCEQUARTER OPENINGBALANCEYEAR	Calculates a value at the calendar end of the period prior to the given period.
TOTALMTD TOTALYTD TOTALQTD	Calculates a value over the interval that starts at the first day of the period and ends at the latest date in the specified date column.
DATEADD	Returns a table that contains a column of dates, shifted either forward or backward in time.
DATESBETWEEN	Returns a table that contains a column of dates that begins with the start_date and continues until the end_date.
DATESINPERIOD	Returns a table that contains a column of dates that begins with the start_date and continues for the specified number_of_intervals.
DATESMDT DATESQTD DATESYTD	Returns a table that contains a column of the dates for the given period in the current context.
ENDOFMONTH ENDOFQUARTER ENDOFYEAR	Returns the last date of the given period in the current context.
NEXTDAY NEXTMONTH NEXTQUARTER NEXTYEAR	Returns a one column table containing all dates in the next period, based on the date specified in the current context.
FIRSTDATE	Returns the first date from the specified column of dates based on the current context.
FIRSTNONBLANK	Returns the first value in the column filtered by the current context where the expression is not blank.
LASTDATE	Returns the last date in the current context for the specified column of dates.

LASTNONBLANK	Returns the last value in the column filtered by the current context where the expression is not blank.
PARALLELPERIOD	Returns a table that contains a column of dates that represents a period parallel to the dates in the specified dates column, in the current context, with the dates shifted a number of intervals either forward in time or back in time.
PREVIOUSDAY PREVIOUSMONTH PREVIOUSQUARTER PREVIOUSYEAR	Returns a one column table containing all dates in the previous period, based on the date specified in the current context.
SAMEPERIODLASTYEAR	Returns a table that contains a column of dates shifted one year back in time from the dates in the specified dates column using the current context.
STARTOFMONTH STARTOFQUARTER STARTOFYEAR	Returns the first date of the specified period based on the current context.

In order to use time intelligence functions in our data model, we need to have a table marked as a date table and identify one of the columns of that table as a unique identifier, which should be of the date data type.

In our data model, we have a Date table defined which can be marked as a date table, and the column FullDateAlternateKey which is a unique identifier for the table and is of the date data type. In our data model, we mark the Date table by selecting the table and clicking **Table** > **Date** > **Mark As Date Table** as shown in the following figure.

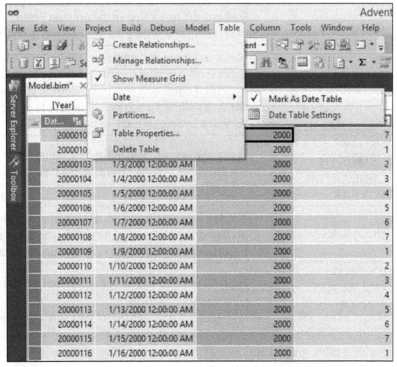

Figure 69: Setting up a table to use time intelligence functions

Next, we click the **Date Table Settings** option in the same menu, and select the **FullDateAlternateKey** unique identifier column in the **Date** field.

Figure 70: Marking a date table

Now that we have marked a date table, we use time intelligence functions to define calculations in our data model.

TotalYTD, TotalQTD, and TotalMTD functions

TotalYTD, TotalQTD, and TotalMTD are functions commonly used in financial analysis to evaluate an expression from the start of the year to the current date, from the start of the quarter to the current date, and from the start of the month to the current date. For example:

```
TOTALYTD(<expression>,<dates>[,<filter>][,<year_end_date>])
TOTALQTD(<expression>,<dates>[,<filter>])
```

In our data model, we define the YTD Sales and QTD Sales measures as follows:

```
YTD Sales:=TOTALYTD(SUM('Reseller
Sales'[SalesAmount]),'Date'[FullDateAlternateKey],ALL('Date'),"6/30")
QTD Sales:=TOTALQTD(SUM('Reseller Sales'[SalesAmount]),
'Date'[FullDateAlternateKey],ALL('Date'))
```

	A	B	C	D
1	Row Labels	Sales	YTD Sales	QTD Sales
2	⊟2002	$16,288,441.77	$16,288,441.77	$4,153,820.42
3	⊟Q1	$3,193,633.97	$3,193,633.97	$3,193,633.97
4	July	$489,328.58	$489,328.58	$489,328.58
5	August	$1,538,408.31	$2,027,736.89	$2,027,736.89
6	September	$1,165,897.08	$3,193,633.97	$3,193,633.97
7	⊞Q2	$4,871,801.34	$8,065,435.31	$4,871,801.34
8	⊞Q3	$4,069,186.04	$12,134,621.34	$4,069,186.04
9	⊟Q4	$4,153,820.42	$16,288,441.77	$4,153,820.42
10	April	$882,899.94	$13,017,521.29	$882,899.94
11	May	$2,269,116.71	$15,286,638.00	$3,152,016.65
12	June	$1,001,803.77	$16,288,441.77	$4,153,820.42
13	⊞2003	$27,921,670.52	$27,921,670.52	/33,903.82
14	⊞2004	$36,240,484.70	$36,240,484.70	$8,935,377.49
15	Grand Total	$80,450,596.98		

Figure 71: Using the TotalYTD and TotalQTD functions

PREVIOUSYEAR, PREVIOUSQUARTER functions

PREVIOUSDAY, PREVIOUSMONTH, PREVIOUSQUARTER, and PREVIOUSYEAR functions are commonly used functions in financial analysis for comparing the current measure value with the previous day, month, quarter, or year. For example:

```
PREVIOUSYEAR(<dates>[,<year_end_date>])
PREVIOUSQUARTER(<dates>)
```

In our data model, we can define the measures PreviousYearSales and PreviousQuarterSales, which calculate the sales for previous years and previous quarters using the following DAX formula:

```
PreviouYearsSales:=CALCULATE([Sales],PreviousYear('Date'[FullDateAlternateK
PreviousQuarterSales:=CALCULATE([Sales],PREVIOUSQUARTER('Date'[FullDateAlte
```

	A	B	C	D
1	Row Labels ▾	Sales	PreviousQuarterSales	PreviousYearSales
2	⊟2002	$16,288,441.77		
3	1	$3,193,633.97		
4	2	$4,871,801.34	$3,193,633.97	
5	3	$4,069,186.04	$4,871,801.34	
6	4	$4,153,820.42	$4,069,186.04	Previous
7	⊟2003	$27,921,670.52	$4,153,820.42	$16,28 Value: No Row: 200
8	1	$8,880,239.44	$4,153,820.42	$16,28 Column:
9	2	$7,041,183.75	$8,880,239.44	$16,288,441.77
10	3	$5,266,343.51	$7,041,183.75	$16,288,441.77
11	4	$6,733,903.82	$5,266,343.51	$16,288,441.77
12	⊟2004	$36,240,484.70	$6,733,903.82	$27,921,670.52
13	1	$10,926,196.09	$6,733,903.82	$27,921,670.52
14	2	$9,276,226.01	$10,926,196.09	$27,921,670.52
15	3	$7,102,685.11	$9,276,226.01	$27,921,670.52
16	4	$8,935,377.49	$7,102,685.11	$27,921,670.52
17	⊟2005		$8,935,377.49	$36,240,484.70
18	1		$8,935,377.49	$36,240,484.70
19	2			$36,240,484.70
20	3			$36,240,484.70
21	4			$36,240,484.70
22	Grand Total	$80,450,596.98		

Figure 72: Using PREVIOUSYEAR and PREVIOUSQUARTER Functions

SAMEPERIODLASTYEAR function

The SAMEPERIODLASTYEAR function returns a table that contains a column of dates shifted one year back in time from the dates in the specified date column, in the current context.

The SAMEPERIODLASTYEAR functionality is also possible by using the PARALLELPERIOD function as follows:

```
PARALLELPERIOD(dates,-1,year)
```

For example:

```
SAMEPERIODLASTYEAR(<dates>)
```

In our data model, we previously defined the calculated measure PreviousSales, which calculates the sales for THE same period last year using the PARALLELPERIOD function as follows:

```
PreviousSales:=CALCULATE([Sales],PARALLELPERIOD('Date'[FullDateAlternateKey
```

We can also rewrite this measure using the SAMEPERIODLASTYEAR function to achieve the same result:

```
PreviousSales:=CALCULATE([Sales],SAMEPERIODLASTYEAR('Date'[FullDateAlternat
```

Now that we are more familiar with DAX functions, in the next section we will see how we can use some of these functions for reporting.

DAX as a query language

In some of the client reporting tools such as SSRS, we use DAX as a query language to define the dataset to fetch the data from the tabular data model cube. When we use DAX as a query language, we use some of the same functions we discussed earlier, which returns a tabular dataset.

When DAX is used as a query language, we use the following syntax:

```
DEFINE
    { MEASURE <table>[<col>] = <expression> }]
EVALUATE <Table Expression>
[ORDER BY {<expression> [{ASC | DESC}]} [, …]
    [START AT {<value>|<parameter>} [, …]] ]
```

DAX as a query language always starts with the EVALUATE keyword followed by an expression, which returns a table. The DEFINE keyword is used to define a calculated measure within the scope of the query.

In order to use DAX as a query language, we use SQL Server Management Studio to connect the tabular Analysis Services cube and click on the **New MDX Query** window.

The same MDX query window is also used to execute DAX queries against tabular model cubes as shown in Figure 73.

For example, the simplest DAX query would be:

```
EVALUATE 'SalesTerritory'
```

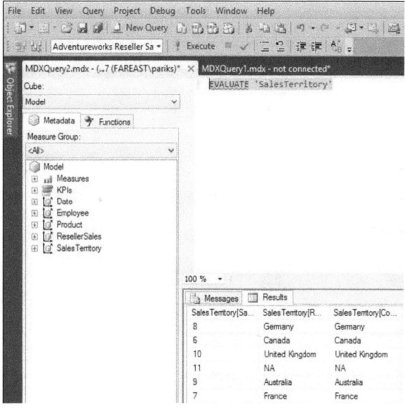

Figure 73: Using DAX as a query language

This query returns SalesTerritory as the output. If the output needs to be sorted by country, we can rewrite the query as:

```
EVALUATE 'SalesTerritory'
ORDER BY 'SalesTerritory'[Country]
```

Applying filters to a DAX query

If we need to evaluate the sales for the fiscal year 2004 for the United States, we use the FILTER function to filter the ResellerSales table for the Country United States and FiscalYear 2004. The resulting DAX query is:

```
EVALUATE
FILTER(
       FILTER('ResellerSales', RELATED('SalesTerritory'[Country])="United
States"),
       RELATED('Date'[FiscalYear])=2004
       )
```

Adding columns to query output in a DAX query

Consider a report where we need all the products in the AdventureWorks catalog along with their max quantities ordered to date. We can use the ADDCOLUMNS function to add a calculated column that computes the max order quantity and adds it to the product table. The resulting DAX query is:

```
EVALUATE
ADDCOLUMNS('Product',
                "Max Quantities
Ordered",CALCULATE(MAX('ResellerSales'[OrderQuantity]),ALL(Product[Product]
                )
ORDER BY [Max Quantities Ordered] desc
```

Aggregating and grouping in a DAX query

Consider a report where we need the aggregated Sales value for each Product Category. This can be easily achieved in a DAX query by using the SUMMARIZE function as follows:

```
EVALUATE
SUMMARIZE(
'Product',
'Product'[Product Category],
"Sales",FORMAT(SUM(ResellerSales[SalesAmount])),"CURRENCY")
)
ORDER BY [Sales] desc
```

Product[Product ...	[Sales]
Bikes	$66,302,381.56
Accessories	$571,297.93
Components	$11,799,076.66
Clothing	$1,777,840.84

Figure 74: Using a DAX query to aggregate values

If we want to compute total sales as well, we can use the SUMMARIZE function along with ROLLUP in the DAX query:

```
EVALUATE
SUMMARIZE (
'Product',
ROLLUP('Product'[Product Category]),
"Sales",FORMAT(SUM(ResellerSales[SalesAmount])),"CURRENCY")
)
ORDER BY [Sales] asc
```

Product[Product ...	[Sales]
Clothing	$1,777,840.84
Components	$11,799,076.66
Accessories	$571,297.93
Bikes	$66,302,381.56
	$80,450,596.98

Figure 75: Using a DAX query to aggregate values

Using CROSSJOIN in a DAX query

Consider a report where we need to compute the sales for each country, for each fiscal year. We can use the CROSSJOIN function to achieve this as shown in the following DAX query:

```
EVALUATE
FILTER(
ADDCOLUMNS(
        CROSSJOIN(
                ALL('Date'[FiscalYear]),
                ALL('SalesTerritory'[Country])
                ),
        "Sales",FORMAT(ResellerSales[Sales],"CURRENCY")
        ),
        ResellerSales[Sales]>0
        )
```

Date[FiscalYear]	SalesTerritory[Co...	[Sales]
2002	United States	$13,083,173.27
2003	United States	$19,129,314.05
2004	United States	$20,479,838.60
2002	Canada	$3,018,750.63
2003	Canada	$2,458,854.76
2004	Canada	$4,058,260.19
2003	France	$1,388,272.61
2004	France	$3,121,616.32
2004	Germany	$1,790,640.23
2004	Australia	$1,421,810.93

Figure 76: Using CROSSJOIN in a DAX query

Using TOPN in a DAX query

Consider a report where we need to identify the top three products that are in demand. To achieve this, we will use the TOPN function and the Demand Rank calculated column defined previously, which calculates the rank for each product based on the total order quantities sold to date.

```
EVALUATE
TOPN(3,Product,Product[Demand Rank],1)
ORDER BY Product[Demand Rank]
```

Product[Product]	Product[Color]	Product[Size]	Product[Weight]	Product[Large Pr...	Product[Product...	Product[Product...	Product[Product...	Product[Demand...
Full-Finger Glov...	Black	.		System.Byte[]	Clothing	Gloves	473	1
Women's Mount...	Black	.		System.Byte[]	Clothing	Shorts	475	2
Women's Mount...	Black	3		System.Byte[]	Clothing	Shorts	474	3

Figure 77: Using the TOPN function in a DAX query

Define measures in a DAX query

In the previous example where we designed a DAX query to calculate the max quantities sold for each product to date, we can rewrite the query by defining the measure as shown in the following sample.

```
DEFINE MEASURE 'Product'[Max Quantities
```

```
Ordered]=CALCULATE(MAX('ResellerSales'[OrderQuantity]),ALL(Product[Product]

EVALUATE
ADDCOLUMNS('Product',
                "Max Quantities Ordered",'Product'[Max Quantities
Ordered]
                )
ORDER BY [Max Quantities Ordered] desc
```

Defining query-scoped measures simplifies the query to a large extent. For instance, in the previous query we first define a calculated measure to compute the max order quantity sold for all products. When this measure is used within the ADDCOLUMNS function, the measure is evaluated in row context for each row of the product table, which gives the max order quantity for each product.

Using the GENERATE function in a DAX query

In the previous example, we calculated the top three products in demand based on the total order quantities sold using TOPN. Now, let us say we need to calculate the top three products in demand for each country to identify the most popular products in each country.

To do this, we need to iterate the same TOPN calculation for each country. This is possible using the GENERATE function in DAX as follows.

```
DEFINE MEASURE 'Product'[Max Quantities
Ordered]=IF(ISBLANK(MAX('ResellerSales'[OrderQuantity])),0,MAX('ResellerSal
EVALUATE
GENERATE
(
VALUES('SalesTerritory'[Country]),
ADDCOLUMNS(
TOPN(3,VALUES('Product'[Product]),'Product'[Max Quantities Ordered]),
            "Max Quantities Ordered",'Product'[Max Quantities Ordered]
    )
)
```

In this DAX query, we repeat the TOPN calculation which calculates the top three products based on the max order quantities sold for each country using the GENERATE function. The resulting output of the query is shown in the following figure:

SalesTerritory[Co...	Product[Product]	[Max Quantities ...
United States	Women's Mount...	40
United States	Full-Finger Glov...	44
United States	Women's Mount...	41
Canada	Women's Mount...	26
Canada	Women's Mount...	27
Canada	Full-Finger Glov...	27
France	AWC Logo Cap	24
France	Classic Vest, S	25
France	Hitch Rack - 4-...	28
Germany	Water Bottle - 3...	22
Germany	Classic Vest, S	36

Figure 78: Using the GENERATE function in a DAX query

These examples should give us enough exposure to get started with DAX. Like with any other query language, we can achieve expertise in DAX with more practice.

Summary

In this chapter, we learned how to define calculated columns and measures using the DAX language. In the next chapter, we will discuss how to prepare our data model for deployment and deploying the data model for reporting and analytics.

Chapter 4 Preparing the Data Model for Reporting and Deployment

Once we have completed the design of the data model and added the required calculated columns and measures using DAX, we next plan and prepare the data model for reporting and deployment. In this chapter, we will learn a few tips to prepare the data model for reporting by hiding undesired columns, creating perspectives, and improving the end user experience. In the latter half of this chapter, we will learn about defining roles, partitions, and deploying the data model to an SSAS instance.

Hiding undesired columns and tables from the data model

In our data model, we import some of the key columns since they are used to define relationships with other tables in the model. Besides key columns, we also import some columns that may not be directly consumed by end users, but are used to define calculated columns. These key columns, called intermediate columns, need not be exposed to end users. If the columns are not used for reporting, they should be hidden from the reporting view to enhance the user experience.

 Note: If the column is not used in the data model at all, it should not be imported, since any redundant columns in the data model add to the processing time and storage and impact the overall performance of the system.

In our data model, we have key columns and a few unused columns that are used for defining relationships or intermediate calculations; we will hide those columns.

In order to hide a column from the data model, we select the table and right-click the column as shown in the following figure.

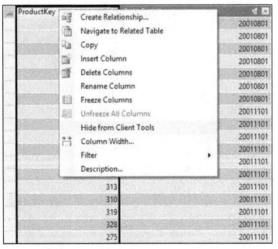

Figure 79: Selecting a column to hide

Click **Hide from Client Tools**, and the column will appear unavailable as shown in the following figure.

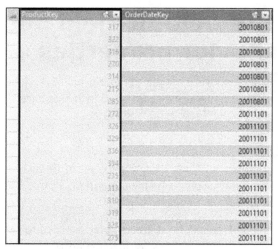

Figure 80: A hidden column

Similarly, if a table is not required for reporting, we can hide it from client tools. To hide a table from client tools, right-click the table's tab and select **Hide from Client Tools**.

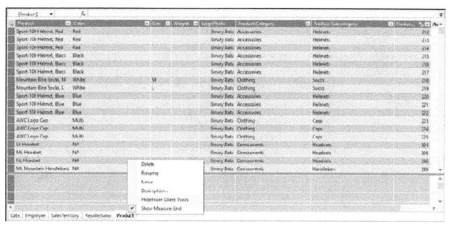

Figure 81: Hiding a table

Once a table or a column is hidden from client tools, it is not visible when users interact with the data model using Excel, Power View, or PPS Dashboards.

Setting the Default Field Set and Table Behavior properties

The tabular data model supports a couple of table properties, default field set and table behavior, which were specifically designed to enhance the user interactivity and experience for the Power View reporting client.

Default field set

The default field set property is used to define the set of fields or columns of the table so that when the end user clicks on the table in the Power View report, the defined column set is reported automatically.

In order to set the default field set for a given table, we need to select the table tab at the bottom in the grid view and press F4 to open the properties window. In the **Properties** window for the SalesTerritory table, we see the table property **Default Field Set** as shown in the following figure.

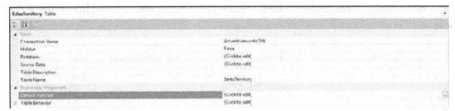

Figure 82: SalesTerritory table properties

When we click the **Click to Edit** cell next to the Default Field Set cell, we can select the default field set as shown in the following figure.

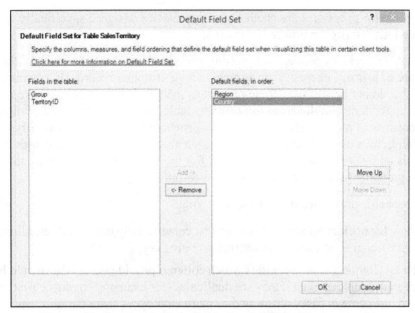

Figure 83: Setting default fields for the SalesTerritory table

We then select **Region** and **Country** as the default fields for the SalesTerritory. Now, when users click on the SalesTerritory table in Power View, the report automatically populates the Region and Country fields.

Figure 84: Power View with default fields

Table Behavior

Table behavior properties are another set of properties designed specifically to enhance interactivity for Power View users.

Setting table behavior properties is recommended for tables where the individual rows are of primary interest, such as employee or customer records. In contrast, tables that do not benefit from these properties include those that act as lookup tables (for example, a date table, a product category table, or a department table, where the table consists of a relatively small number of rows and columns), or summary tables containing rows that are only relevant when summarized (for example, census data that rolls up by gender, age, or geography). For lookup and summary tables, the default grouping behavior produces the best result.

Table behavior properties include the following:

- **Row Identifier**: Specifies a column that contains only unique values, allowing that column to be used as an internal grouping key.
- **Keep Unique Rows**: Specifies which columns provide values that should be treated as unique even if they are duplicates (for example, employee first name and last name in cases where two or more employees share the same name).
- **Default Label**: Specifies which column provides a display name to represent row data (for example, employee name in an employee record).
- **Default Image**: Specifies which column provides an image that represents the row data (for example, a photo ID in an employee record).

In our data model we have a Products table which will generally be reported as individual records, and hence would be a good candidate for using table behavior properties.

In the grid view (also called the data view), we click on the **Product** table tab at the bottom and press F4. We see table behavior properties just below the default field set properties. In the table behavior properties for **Product Table**, we set the following values:

Row Identifier: ProductKey
Keep Unique Rows: Product
Default Label: Product
Default Image: LargePhoto

Setting the Data Category property for columns

In the tabular data model, we can classify some of the column data into a set of predefined categories. These properties are useful for client tools like Power View, which can use these properties to report the data with the best possible visualization.

In our data model, we have a SalesTerritory table with a Country column; we can set the Data category of the Country column to **Country**. To change the Data Category property for the Country column, select the column and press F4 to open the Properties window, as shown in the following figure:

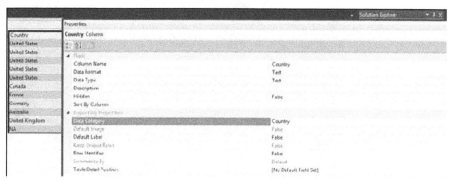

Figure 85: Country column properties

After setting the Data Category for the Country column, when we browse the data model in Power View, we see the map icon next to the Country column.

Figure 86: Map icon next to Country column

Power View uses these Data Category values to map the data with the best visualization available for that type of data.

Similarly, we can classify other columns if the data in the column matches the set of predefined data category available.

Setting the Data Category property for Columns

Setting the Format property for measures

In the previous chapter, we defined various calculated measures (Sales, Cost, Profit, Margin, etc.). When these calculated measures are used as-is in an Excel or Power View report, they will not make much sense to the end user since the measures will be reported in a plain number format. It is important for us to set the Format property for measures specifying whether the format of the measure should be a currency or percentage.

In our data model, we have defined the Sales measure using the following DAX formula.

```
Sales:=SUM(ResellerSales[SalesAmount])
```

When this DAX measure is used as is in a Power View or Excel report, we will see the following report.

Row Labels	Sales
⊟Accessories	571297.9278
⊞Bike Racks	7736.156
⊞Bottles and Cages	7476.6036
⊞Cleaners	11188.3725
⊞Helmets	258712.9323
⊞Hydration Packs	65518.7485
⊞Locks	16225.22
⊞Pumps	13514.6873
⊞Tires and Tubes	925.2076
⊞Bikes	66302381.56
⊞Clothing	1777840.839
⊞Components	11799076.66
Grand Total	80450596.98

Figure 87: Sales measure without a data format

In order to set the Format property for the Sales measure, select the **Sales Measure** cell in the measure grid and press F4 to open the Properties window. In the Properties window, we set the **Format** property to **Currency** as shown in the following figure.

Figure 88: Setting the Format property

We can further specify the number of decimal places, which is set to **2** by default, and **Currency Symbol** for localization purposes.

Similarly, we can define the properties for other measures to appropriately format values before we deploy the data model.

Setting the Summarize property for columns

In the tabular data model, we can set the default aggregation for the column so that whenever the column is checked in the Power View report, it automatically aggregates the data.

However, if the column is of numeric data type, the default aggregation for the column is set to **Sum**, which may be undesired at times. For example, when we browse the data model in Power View and expand the Date table, we see the following:

Figure 89: Date table with summation columns

In order to ensure these columns do not have the summation sign next to them, press F4 to open the Properties window for that column and select **Do not summarize** for the **Summarize By** property as shown in the following figure.

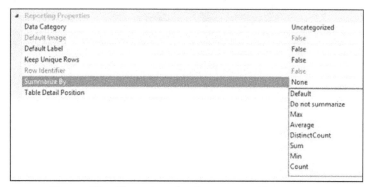

Figure 90: Changing the Summarize By property

We need to select **Do not summarize** for all the columns with whole number data types that we do not want to aggregate. For the columns we wish to aggregate, we can select from the default aggregations in the Properties window for each column.

Adding descriptions for columns, tables, and measures

In the tabular data model, we can add descriptions to columns, tables, and calculated measures. These descriptions might be a helpful tip for the end users or analysts, informing them what the column, table, or measure is meant for and what data it will display. The description is shown as a tooltip in the Power View report.

In our data model, we can add descriptions to a table, column, or field by right-clicking on it and clicking **Description** as shown in the following figure.

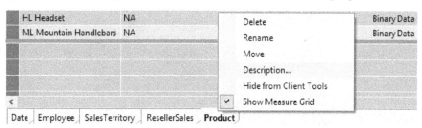

Figure 91: Adding a description to a table

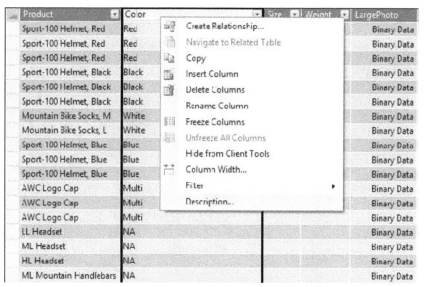

Figure 92: Adding a description to a column

Figure 93: Adding a description to a field

The description we write will appear as a tooltip for end users in the Power View report:

Figure 94: Field description

Descriptions are useful by providing additional information about the column, table, or calculated fields, which can enhance the user's reporting experience.

Defining perspectives

A tabular data model can contain multiple data marts together in a single database to avoid redundancy for shared dimension tables. Therefore, a single data model can have a large number of tables, columns, and measures defined. If all these columns and measures are exposed to the end user via reporting clients like Excel or Power View, it will be overwhelming for end users. In order to improve the user experience so that users can see only the tables, columns, and measures that are relevant to them for analysis, we can define perspectives.

Perspectives are similar to views in RDBMS, which act as windows to the data model, displaying the fields that are relevant for analysis. We can define multiple perspectives in the data model based on the end user's need for analysis.

In our data model, in order to define perspectives, we click the **Perspectives** button on the toolbar as shown in the following figure:

Figure 95: Perspectives option

The Perspectives wizard will appear. When we click on **New Perspective**, we can provide a name to the new perspective defined and use the check boxes to include the columns, hierarchies, measures, and tables needed. In our data model, we define the perspective "Reseller Sales" as shown in the following figure.

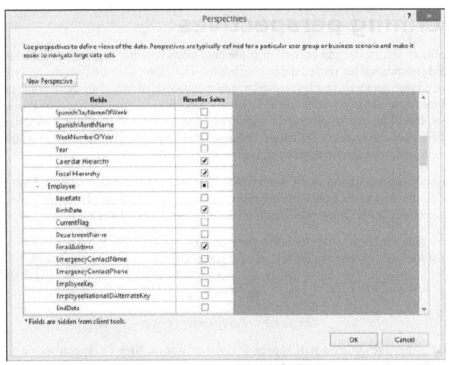

Figure 96: Defining a new perspective

To create the "Reseller Sales" perspective, we select the following columns and fields from each table.

Table	Fields Included in Reseller Sales Perspective
Date	Calendar Hierarchy, Fiscal Hierarchy
Employee	Name, BirthDate, EmailAddress, Gender, Marital Status
Product	Products, Color, Size, LargePhoto
ResellerSales	Sales, OrderQuantity, % Geography Contribution, Profit, Revised Sales Target, YoY, YoY %
SalesTerritory	Geography

For the Date, Product, and SalesTerritory tables, we have included the hierarchy we defined earlier in the perspective instead of selecting the individual columns to avoid redundancy.

In order to connect to the perspective, the end user needs to specify the perspective name while defining the connection string for the data model.

After deploying the model in Excel, we will define the data connection in the Data

Connection Wizard. The wizard gives us an option to select the perspective, as shown in the following figure.

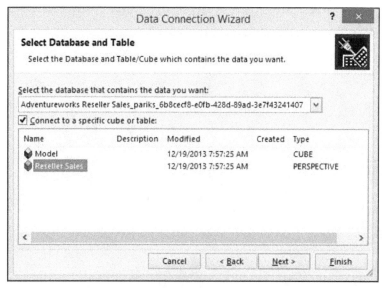

Figure 97: Connecting to a perspective

When end users connect to the Reseller Sales perspective, the fields we included in defining the perspective are displayed as shown in the following figure.

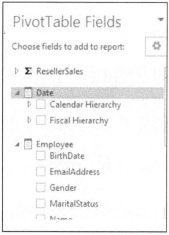

Figure 98: Reseller Sales perspective fields

For large data models or cubes, it is always recommended to define multiple perspectives to provide end users only the fields required for their analysis.

Defining roles and security

The SSAS tabular model uses role-based security where a valid authenticated user would see the data, depending on the roles the user belongs to. Like the multidimensional model, the SSAS tabular model supports Windows authentication (the only authentication supported). Unlike the multidimensional model (which has cell security and dimension security) used to restrict the user at cell-level and dimension members respectively, the tabular model has row-level security where we can restrict the users to the rows of the table which they can view. Row filters also apply to related tables; for example, if a row is restricted in the Product table, the row in the Reseller Sales table corresponding to the restricted row in the Product table will also be restricted.

Roles are used in Microsoft SQL Server Analysis Services to manage security for Analysis Services and data. There are two types of roles in Analysis Services:

- The server role: A fixed role that provides administrator access to an instance of Analysis Services.
- Database roles: Roles defined by model authors and administrators to control access to a model database and data for non-administrator users.

Roles defined for a tabular model are database roles. That is, the roles contain members consisting of Windows users or groups that have specific permissions that define the actions those members can perform in the model database. A database role is created as a separate object in the database, and applies only to the database in which that role is created. Windows users, Windows groups, or both are included in the role by the model author, who, by default, has administrator permissions on the workspace database server. In a deployed model, the roles are managed by an administrator.

Roles in tabular models can be further defined with row filters. Row filters use DAX expressions to define the rows in a table, and any related rows that a user can query. Row filters using DAX expressions can only be defined for the Read and Read and Process permissions.

By default, when you create a new tabular model project, the project does not have any roles. You can define roles using the Role Manager in SQL Server Data Tools. When roles are defined during model authoring, they are applied to the model workspace database. When the model is deployed, the same roles are applied to the deployed model. After a model has been deployed, members of the server role (Analysis Services administrators) and database administrators can manage the roles associated with the model and the members associated with each role by using SQL Server Management Studio.

In our data model, we need to define security such that each country's users should see the sales data specific to their region, while top-level management should have unrestricted access to all the data. In other words, we need to define roles for each country to restrict the data to that country and further assign users to roles based on the country they belong to.

To define roles in our data model, click the **Roles** button in the toolbar as shown in the following figure.

Figure 99: Roles option

This launches the Role Manager. Click **New** to create a new role. By default, the name of the new role created is "Role." Click on the role to rename it to **United States**, which is meant for all users who are allowed to view U.S. sales transactions.

When we click on the **Permissions** drop-down, we see the following options.

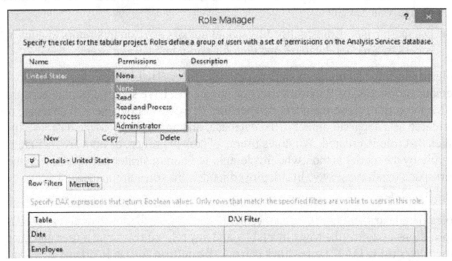

Figure 100: Permissions options in the Role Manager

The permissions options are similar to those in the multidimensional model.

Permissions	Description	Row filters using DAX
None	Members cannot make any modifications to the model database schema and cannot query data.	Row filters do not apply. No data is visible to users in this role.
Read	Members are allowed to query data based on row filters but cannot see the model database in SSMS, cannot make any	Row filters can be applied. Only data specified in the row

		filter DAX formula is visible to users.
Read and Process	Members are allowed to query data based on row-level filters and run process operations by running a script or package that contains a process command, but cannot make any changes to the database. Cannot view the model database in SQL Server Management Studio.	Row filters can be applied. Only data specified in the row filter DAX formula can be queried.
Process	Members can run process operations by running a script or package that contains a process command. Cannot modify the model database schema. Cannot query data. Cannot query the model database in SQL Server Management Studio.	Row filters do not apply. No data can be queried in this role.
Administrator	Members can make modifications to the model schema and can query all data in the model designer, reporting client, and SQL Server Management Studio.	Row filters do not apply. All data can be queried in this role.

In our data model, we define permissions and a description for the role, and add a DAX filter as shown in the following figure.

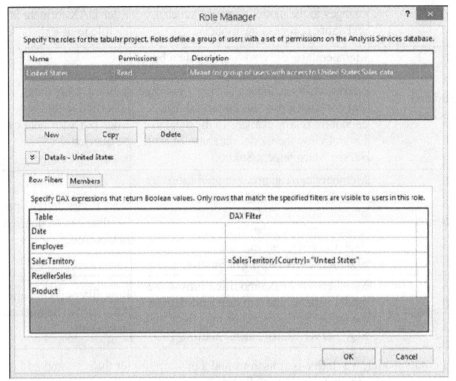

Figure 101: Defining a role

The DAX filter used to define the role is nothing but a DAX expression that is evaluated in row context (similar to calculated columns) and returns Boolean values of True or False. In the previous role definition, the DAX filter is evaluated for each row of the SalesTerritory table; for the rows where the country is the United States, it returns True, while for all other rows it returns False.

To assign Windows groups or individual users to this role, click the **Members** tab next to the Row Filters tab and click **Add** to add the Windows user or group.

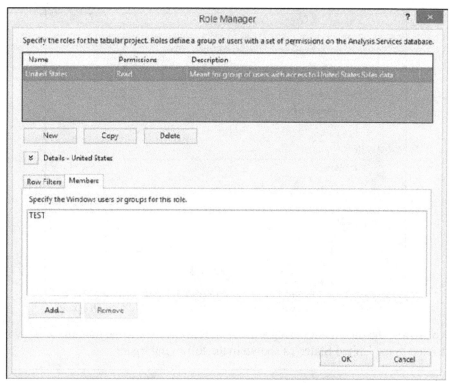

Figure 102: Adding members to the role

Similarly, we need to define the role for each country. To expedite development, we can click the **Copy** button in the Role Manager wizard, which will create a duplicate copy of the United States role that we defined earlier. In the copy, we can modify the DAX filter to a different country name and add members who belong to the role.

 Note: If a member is part of multiple roles, he or she will inherit the permissions of both roles. If a member is part of multiple roles and one role denies a permission while another role allows the permission, the user will be allowed the permission.

To test the role, connect to the data model using Excel by clicking **Analyze in Excel** in the toolbar as shown in the following figure.

Figure 103: Analyze in Excel

We get an option to connect to the model as the current Windows user, other Windows user, or a role-defined user. Choose the **Role** option and select **United States** from the drop-down list as shown in the following figure.

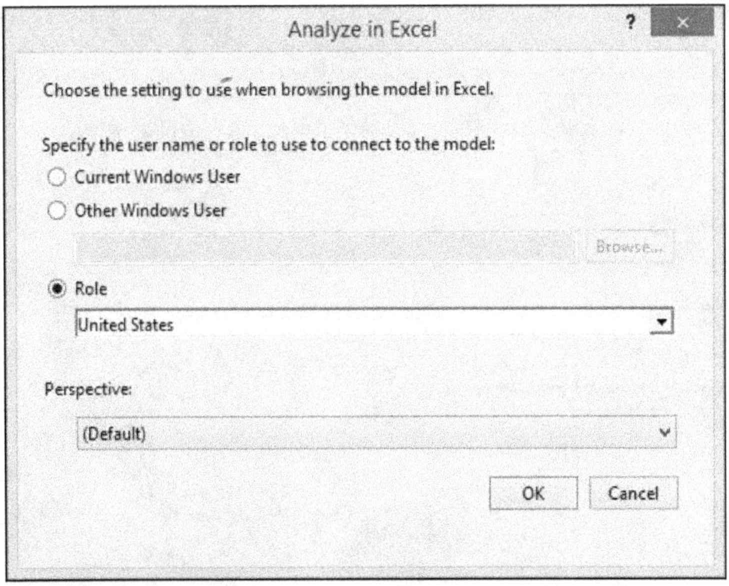

Figure 104: Choose the role to use when analyzing in Excel

If we browse the data model using a pivot table, we will see the data in the table is restricted to the United States as shown in the following figure.

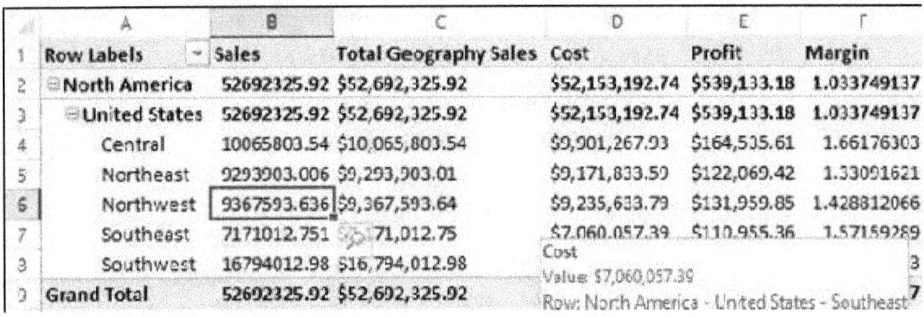

	A	B	C	D	E	F
1	Row Labels ▾	Sales	Total Geography Sales	Cost	Profit	Margin
2	North America	52692325.92	$52,692,325.92	$52,153,192.74	$539,133.18	1.033749137
3	United States	52692325.92	$52,692,325.92	$52,153,192.74	$539,133.18	1.033749137
4	Central	10065803.54	$10,065,803.54	$9,901,267.93	$164,535.61	1.66176303
5	Northeast	9293903.006	$9,293,903.01	$9,171,833.59	$122,069.42	1.33091621
6	Northwest	9367593.636	$9,367,593.64	$9,235,633.79	$131,959.85	1.428812066
7	Southeast	7171012.751	$7,171,012.75	$7,060,057.39	$110,955.36	1.57159289
8	Southwest	16794012.98	$16,794,012.98			
9	Grand Total	52692325.92	$52,692,325.92			

Cost
Value: $7,060,057.39
Row: North America - United States - Southeast

Figure 105: Data model restricted to United States data

Dynamic security

Dynamic security provides a way to define row-level security based on the user name of the user currently logged in or the CustomData property returned from a connection string. In order to implement dynamic security, you must include in your model a table with login values (Windows user names) for users as well as a field that can be used to define a particular permission; for example, a DimEmployees table with a login ID (domain and username) as well as a Country value for each employee.

To implement dynamic security, you can use the following functions as part of a DAX formula to return the user name of the user currently logged in, or the CustomData property in a connection string:

Function	Description
USERNAME Function (DAX)	Returns the domain and username of the user currently logged on.
CUSTOMDATA Function (DAX)	Returns the CustomData property in a connection string.

We can use the LOOKUPVALUE function to return values for a column in which the Windows user name is the same as the user name returned by the USERNAME function or a string returned by the CustomData function. Queries can then be restricted where the values returned by LOOKUPVALUE match values in the same or a related table. For example:

```
='Sales Territory'[Country]=LOOKUPVALUE('Employee Security'[Country],
'Employee Security'[Login Id], USERNAME(), 'Employee Security'[Country],
'Sales Territory'[Country])
```

 Note: This formula was written for a customized version of the AdventureWorksDW2012 database and will not work as is for the sample AdventureWorksDW2012 database.

For more information on setting dynamic security, you can refer to the following white paper from Cathy Dumas, the program manager for SSAS Team during the SQL 2012 release: http://msdn.microsoft.com/en-us/library/jj127437.aspx.

Defining partitions

Partitions in tabular models divide a table into logical partition objects. Each partition can then be processed independent of other partitions. For example, a table may include certain row sets that contain data that rarely changes, but other row sets have data that changes often. In these cases, there is no need to process all of the data when you really just want to process a portion of the data. Partitions enable you to divide portions of data you need to process frequently from the data that can be processed less frequently.

Effective model design utilizes partitions to eliminate unnecessary processing and subsequent processor load on Analysis Services servers, while making sure that data is processed and refreshed often enough to reflect the most recent data from data sources. One of the objectives of using partition tables in our data model is to expedite data refreshing in the model.

In our data model, we have the Reseller Sales table, which currently contains around 65,000 records. These can be processed pretty quickly, but during the development of the data model, one has to also take into account the growth of the data warehouse in the coming years. In most data models, fact or transaction tables are good candidates for partitioning, as the data grows daily. However, partitioning is not restricted to fact tables, and can be applied to dimension tables as well.

In most data models, we might also prefer to partition by date or time since in most cases after the transaction enters the data warehouse, there are rare chances to update or delete the transaction. Hence we design the yearly partition for the previous year, while for the current year we can design a monthly partition to minimize the processing requirements.

To define partitions, select the relevant table and click the **Partitions** button in the toolbar as shown in the following figure.

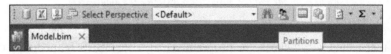

Figure 106: Partitions button

This will launch the Partition Manager window.

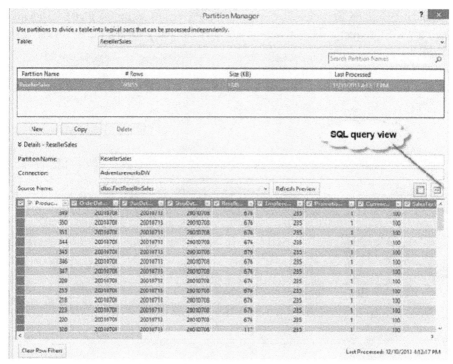

Figure 107: Partition Manager

The Partition Manager exposes the current partition for the Reseller Sales Table, which is a single partition with all the records.

We choose to partition the Reseller Sales table using OrderDateKey in Fiscal Calendar. The minimum OrderDateKey value available in our FactResellerSales table is 20010701, while the maximum OrderDateKey value available is 20040601. We divide the table into five partitions using the OrderDateKey in Fiscal Calendar as shown in the following table.

Partition Name	Partition Logic
FY01 Sales	OrderDateKey < 20010701
FY02 Sales	OrderDateKey between 20010701 and 20020630
FY03 Sales	OrderDateKey between 20020701 and 20030630
FY04 Sales	OrderDatekey between 20030701 and 20040630
FY05 Sales	OrderDatekey > 20040630

In order to define the first partition, change the **Partition Name** to **FY01 Sales** and switch to the SQL query view, where we define the query for the partition as:

```
SELECT [dbo].[FactResellerSales].* FROM [dbo].[FactResellerSales]
Where OrderDateKey < 20010701
```

Figure 108: Adding the FY01 Sales partition

Next, click **Copy** to create another partition, which we name **FY02 Sales** and modify the query as:

```
SELECT [dbo].[FactResellerSales].* FROM [dbo].[FactResellerSales]
Where OrderDateKey between 20010701 and 20020630
```

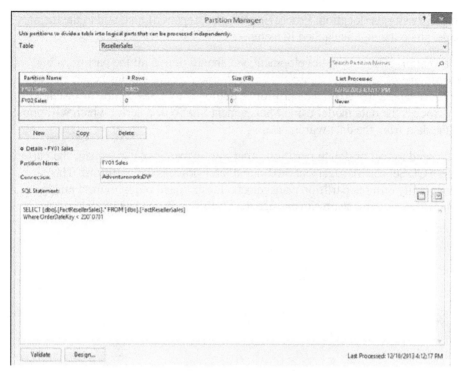

Figure 109: Adding the FY02 Sales partition

Similarly, we define the partitions FY03 Sales, FY04 Sales, and FY05 Sales. While defining partitions, we need to ensure there isn't an overlap between the partitions, and that we haven't missed any rows from the fact table; otherwise we will get incorrect calculation results.

Once we have all the partitions defined, we can either process all the partitions at once by clicking **Process Table**, or process one partition at a time by clicking **Process Partitions**.

 Note: The Process All option processes the entire data model, so if other tables are already processed, we might not want to use this option.

Figure 110: Process options

While developing the data model, it is always recommended to define all partitions, but not process all partitions. When we process the partitions while developing the data model in SSDT, the data is stored in the workspace database, which is like a temporary storage location. Processing the partitions will also add to the memory usage, since the data is cached in memory.

As a best practice during development, we should define all the partitions but process one of the smallest partitions and define the calculations based on that partition data. Later when the partition is deployed to a SSAS tabular instance, we can process the data model using Management Studio or a script which will populate all the data from the data warehouse.

If we need to add or delete partitions after deployment, we can manage the partitions using SQL Server Management Studio and later process the partitions. This functionality ensures partition management doesn't need redeployment and even administrators in the team can manage the partitions in the data model.

Deploying the data model

Once we have completed the design and development of the tabular data model, it is time to deploy the model to the SSAS tabular instance.

There are several methods you can use to deploy a tabular model project. Most of the deployment methods that can be used for other Analysis Services projects, such as the multidimensional method, can also be used to deploy tabular model projects.

Method	Description
Deploy command in SQL Server Data Tools	The deploy command provides a simple and intuitive method to deploy a tabular model project from the SQL Server Data Tools environment.
Analysis Management Objects (AMO) automation	AMO provides a programmatic interface to the complete command set for Analysis Services, including commands that can be used for solution deployment. As an approach for solution deployment, AMO automation is the most flexible, but it also requires some programming effort. A key advantage to using AMO is that you can use SQL Server Agent with your AMO application to run deployment on a preset schedule.
XMLA	Use SQL Server Management Studio to generate an XMLA script of the metadata of an existing Analysis Services database, and then run that script on another server to recreate the initial database. XMLA scripts are easily formed in SQL Server Management Studio by defining the deployment process, and then codifying it and saving it in an XMLA script. Once you have the XMLA script in a saved file, you can easily run the script according to a schedule, or embed the script in an application that connects directly to an instance of Analysis Services. You can also run XMLA Scripts on a preset basis using SQL Server Agent, but you do not have the same flexibility with XMLA scripts as with AMO. AMO provides a wider breadth of functionality by hosting the complete spectrum of administrative commands.
	Use the Deployment Wizard to use the XMLA output files generated by an Analysis Services project to deploy the project's metadata to a destination server. With the Deployment Wizard, you can deploy directly from the Analysis Services file, as created by the output directory

Deployment Wizard	by the project build.
	The primary advantage of using the Analysis Services Deployment Wizard is convenience. Just as you can save an XMLA script for later use in SQL Server Management Studio, you can save Deployment Wizard scripts. The Deployment Wizard can be run both interactively and at the command prompt via the Deployment Utility.
Deployment utility	The Deployment utility lets you start the Analysis Services deployment engine from a command prompt.
Synchronize Database Wizard	Use the Synchronize Database Wizard to synchronize the metadata and data between any two Analysis Services databases.
	The Synchronize Wizard can be used to copy both data and metadata from a source server to a destination server. If the destination server does not have a copy of the database that you want to deploy, a new database is copied to the destination server. If the destination server already has a copy of the same database, the database on the destination server is updated to use the metadata and data of the source database.
Backup and restore	Backup offers the simplest approach to transferring Analysis Services databases. From the Backup dialog box, you can set the configuration options, and then you can run the backup from the dialog box itself. Or, you can create a script that can be saved and run as frequently as required.
	Backup and restore is not used as frequently as the other deployment methods, but it is a way to quickly complete a deployment with minimal infrastructure requirements.

In this chapter, we will use the first method of deploying the data model using SSDT.

Important: Before we deploy the data model, we must change the data source connection for the data model to point to the production data warehouse.

In order to deploy the data model, we need to set some of the deployment properties. Right-click the project name in **Solution Explorer** and select **Properties** as shown in the following figure.

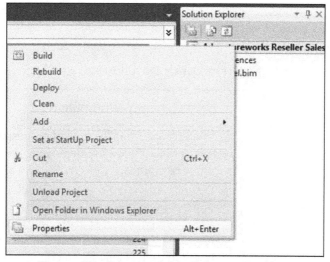

Figure 111: Data model in Solution Explorer

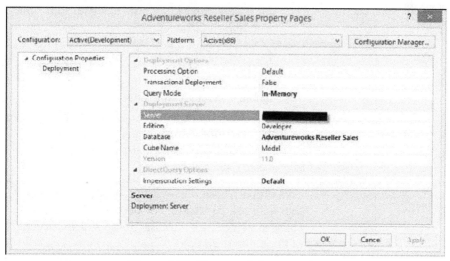

Figure 112: Data model properties

When you deploy the data model, a connection to the Analysis Services instance specified in the **Server** property is established. A new model database with the name specified in the **Database** property is then created on that instance if one does not already exist. Metadata from the model project's Model.bim file is used to configure objects in the model database on the deployment server. With the **Processing** option, you can specify whether only the model metadata is deployed, creating the model database. If **Default** or **Full** is specified, impersonation credentials used to connect to data sources are passed in-memory from the model workspace database to the deployed model database. Analysis Services then runs processing to populate data into the deployed model. Once the deployment process is complete, client applications can connect to the model using a data connection or by using a .bism connection file in SharePoint.

The deployment options properties include the following.

Property	Default Setting	Description
Processing Option	Default	This property specifies the type of processing required when changes to objects are deployed. This property has the following options: • Default: Analysis Services will determine the type of processing required. Unprocessed objects will be processed, and if required, attribute relationships, attribute hierarchies, user hierarchies, and calculated columns will be recalculated. This setting generally results in a faster deployment time than using the Full processing option. • Do Not Process: Only the metadata will be deployed. After deploying, it may be necessary to run a process operation on the deployed model to update and recalculate data. • Full: Both the metadata is deployed and a process full operation is performed. This assures that the deployed model has the most recent updates to both metadata and data.
Transactional Deployment	False	This property specifies whether the deployment is transactional. By default, the deployment of all or changed objects is not transactional with the processing of those deployed objects. Deployment can succeed and persist even if processing fails. You can change this to incorporate deployment and processing in a single transaction.
		This property specifies whether the source from which query results are returned is running in in-memory (cached) mode or in DirectQuery mode. This property has the following options: • DirectQuery: Specifies all queries to the model should use the relational data source only. The DirectQuery mode requires Impersonate settings to be set to specify the credentials used to authenticate

Query Mode	In-Memory	while making a connection to the relational data source • DirectQuery with In-Memory: Specifies that, by default, queries should be answered by using the relational source, unless otherwise specified in the connection string from the client. • In-Memory: Specifies that queries should be answered by using the cache only. • In-Memory with DirectQuery: Specifies that, by default, queries should be answered by using the cache, unless otherwise specified in the connection string from the client.

After setting the deployment properties, right-click on the project again in the Solution Explorer and click **Deploy** to deploy the data model to the SSAS tabular instance specified in the Server property. After deployment is completed successfully, we see the following screen.

Figure 113: Successful deployment

We can further verify the deployment by logging into the target server and connecting to the SSAS tabular instance using SSMS as shown in the following figure.

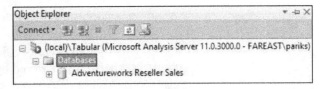

Figure 114: Successful deployment as shown in SSMS

Post-deployment tasks

After the data model has been deployed, we need to complete certain post-deployment tasks:

- Ensure the data source is pointing to the production data warehouse and not the development data warehouse, which can happen if we forget to update the data source before deployment.
- Process the data model if the model was deployed with the Do Not Process option.
- Create a process plan and job to process the table or partition frequently to ensure the data is up to date.
- Assign Windows users or groups to the appropriate roles to give them the right access and permissions to the data model.
- Create or add partitions to the table using Management Studio to minimize the data to process and improve the data refresh time.

Summary

In the next chapter, we will discuss how to use Power View to explore the data model and create visually appealing reports, which can help end users derive meaningful information from their data model.

Chapter 5 Exploring the Data Model with Power View

In the previous chapters we learned how to design, develop, and deploy a data model using SSAS tabular model. In this chapter, we learn how to explore the data model using a reporting tool introduced in SQL 2012: Power View. Power View is a new, Silverlight-based ad hoc reporting tool with a rich set of visualizations useful for data exploration and analysis.

When Power View was introduced with SQL 2012, it was only available in the SharePoint Integrated Mode supported by SharePoint 2010 and SharePoint 2013. With the introduction of Excel 2013, Power View (and PowerPivot) is now natively integrated in Excel as a COM add-in, and is available for reporting. An Excel 2013 worksheet with a Power View report can be uploaded to a SharePoint 2013 document library, and can be rendered by Excel Services (Excel Web app) with SharePoint in the browser as well.

The interfaces for Power View in SharePoint and Excel 2013 are similar. In this chapter, we will be designing Power View reports using Excel 2013, but most of the steps discussed here also hold true for SharePoint.

Creating a connection to the data model in Excel 2013

The first step in designing reports is always creating a data connection to the model. In Excel 2013, we click on the **Data** tab in the toolbar and select **Analysis Services** from the **Other Sources** button as shown in the following figure.

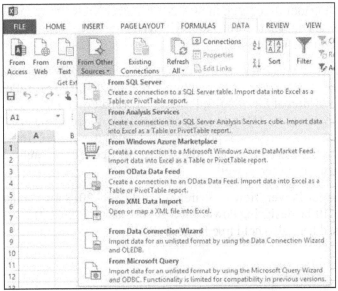

Figure 115: Connecting Excel to Analysis Services

In the Data Connection Wizard, we provide the SSAS instance name under the **Server Name** and use Windows authentication. On the next screen, we select the database from the drop-down list and select the cube or perspective from the data model we intend to connect to, as shown in the following figure.

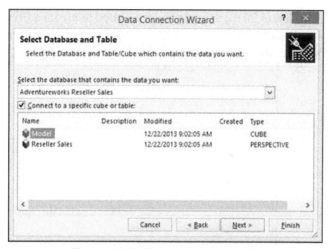

Figure 116: Connecting to a cube

The final screen of the wizard is used to provide the file name, location for the .odc file, and a brief description about the data model. We can also choose the authentication settings to be used if the Excel file is uploaded in a SharePoint document library and is to be viewed in a browser using the Excel web app.

Figure 117: Setting up authentication details

When we click **Finish**, we have the option to import the data model to an Excel workbook. Prior to Excel 2013, we only had the option to create a PivotTable or PivotChart report. With Excel 2013, we also see the Power View report option. Select **Power View** as shown in the following figure.

Figure 118: Creating a Power View report in Excel

We can click the **Properties** button to modify the data refresh settings, which specify when to refresh the data in the Excel worksheet, and other OLAP settings in the Usage tab. In the Definition tab, we see the connection string, which we specified earlier.

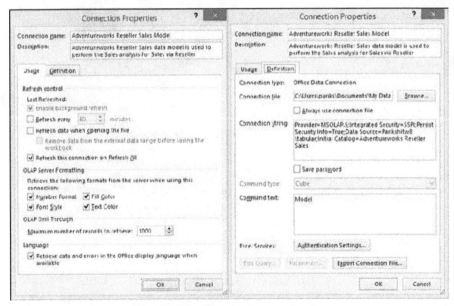

Figure 119: Connection properties

Click **OK** to close the Properties window, and then click **OK** again with the **Power**

View Report option selected to create a Power View report in a separate worksheet as shown in the following figure.

Figure 120: New Power View report

For Power View in SharePoint, we need to create a BISM connection file, which again defines the connection string to the data model.

Power View visualization

Power View is designed to be highly intuitive with rich visualizations such that users should be able design a report with a few clicks, and the data format itself should identify the best visualization available to represent it. This is possible only if we set the right properties, including the default field set, table behavior, format, summarize, and data category, which we discussed in Chapter 4.

In the following sections we discuss all the visualization options available with Power View, and which data type best fits each visualization.

Visualizing data with tables in Power View

One of the simplest and most essential data visualization tools in reporting is table visualization, since most structured data can be best analyzed and interpreted in tabular format. By default, Power View represents most data types in tabular format, which we can later switch to other visualization methods if required.

In order to visualize the data, we first need to select the data in an order from the field list on the right side of the Power View report. First, we select the Products hierarchy followed by the Sales and Profit measures as shown in the following figure.

Figure 121: Selecting data to visualize

The resulting table report in the Power View workspace window appears as shown in Figure 122.

Product_Category	Product_Subcategory	Product	Sales	Profit
Accessories	Bike Racks	Hitch Rack - 4-Bike	$197,736.16	$70,366.72
Accessories	Bottles and Cages	Water Bottle - 30 oz.	$7,476.60	$2,678.35
Accessories	Cleaners	Bike Wash - Dissolver	$11,188.37	$4,019.75
Accessories	Helmets	Sport-100 Helmet, Black	$87,915.37	$29,060.94
Accessories	Helmets	Sport-100 Helmet, Blue	$91,052.87	$29,942.89
Accessories	Helmets	Sport-100 Helmet, Red	$79,744.70	$26,343.08
Accessories	Hydration Packs	Hydration Pack - 70 oz.	$65,518.75	$23,810.29
Accessories	Locks	Cable Lock	$16,225.22	$5,025.85
Accessories	Pumps	Minipump	$13,514.69	$4,196.82
Accessories	Tires and Tubes	Patch Kit/8 Patches	$925.21	$347.93
Bikes	Mountain Bikes	Mountain-100 Black, 38	$1,174,622.74	($26,871.01)
Bikes	Mountain Bikes	Mountain-100 Black, 42	$1,102,848.18	($15,129.42)
Bikes	Mountain Bikes	Mountain-100 Black, 44	$1,163,352.98	($9,669.36)
Bikes	Mountain Bikes	Mountain-100 Black, 48	$1,041,901.60	($19,133.17)
Bikes	Mountain Bikes	Mountain-100 Silver, 38	$1,094,669.28	($22,028.89)
Bikes	Mountain Bikes	Mountain-100 Silver, 42	$1,042,606.27	($9,001.90)

Figure 122: Table visualization in Power View

By default, table visualization sums up the rows and displays the total at the bottom of the table as shown in the following figure.

Bikes	Road Bikes	Road-350-W Yellow, 40	$1,238,754.64	($93,815.17)
Bikes	Touring Bikes	Touring-1000 Yellow, 50	$621,193.28	($121,257.61)
Bikes	Road Bikes	Road-650 Red, 44	$883,173.37	($122,093.35)
Bikes	Road Bikes	Road-350-W Yellow, 48	$1,380,253.88	($124,435.02)
Bikes	Touring Bikes	Touring-1000 Yellow, 46	$1,016,312.83	($218,141.44)
Bikes	Touring Bikes	Touring-1000 Yellow, 60	$1,184,363.30	($259,044.21)
Total			**$80,450,596.98**	**$470,482.60**

Figure 123: Summary rows in table data visualization

If we don't want the total in the report, we can open the **Design** tab on the ribbon, click **Totals**, and select **None**.

Figure 124: Turning off totals

If we need to sort the table based on any column, we click on the column header, which sorts the table in ascending order. Clicking on the column header again sorts the table in descending order.

Product_Subcategory	Product	Sales	Profit
Mountain Bikes	Mountain-200 Black, 38	$3,105,726.66	$282,344.66
Mountain Bikes	Mountain-200 Black, 42	$2,646,352.67	$242,041.15
Mountain Bikes	Mountain-200 Silver, 38	$2,354,215.24	$218,267.98
Mountain Bikes	Mountain-200 Silver, 42	$2,181,044.29	$202,477.14
Mountain Bikes	Mountain-200 Silver, 46	$2,133,156.84	$200,466.78
Mountain Bikes	Mountain-200 Black, 46	$1,936,203.67	$181,466.77
Road Bikes	Road-250 Black, 44	$1,888,480.05	($68,123.97)
Road Bikes	Road-250 Black, 48	$1,656,449.69	($58,621.71)
Road Bikes	Road-350-W Yellow, 48	$1,380,253.88	($124,435.02)
Touring Bikes	Touring-1000 Blue, 60	$1,370,784.22	($71,141.35)
Road Bikes	Road-250 Black, 52	$1,278,046.58	($43,297.55)
Road Bikes	Road-350-W Yellow, 40	$1,238,754.64	($93,815.17)
Touring Bikes	Touring-1000 Yellow, 60	$1,184,363.30	($259,044.21)
Mountain Bikes	Mountain-100 Black, 38	$1,174,622.74	($26,871.01)
Touring Bikes	Touring-1000 Blue, 46	$1,164,973.18	($57,625.58)
Mountain Bikes	Mountain-100 Black, 44	$1,163,352.98	($9,669.36)
Mountain Bikes	Mountain-100 Black, 42	$1,102,848.18	($15,129.42)
Road Bikes	Road-250 Red, 44	$1,096,280.08	($44,328.51)
Mountain Bikes	Mountain-100 Silver, 38	$1,094,669.28	($22,028.89)
Mountain Bikes	Mountain-100 Silver, 44	$1,050,610.85	($4,898.38)
Mountain Bikes	Mountain-100 Silver, 42	$1,043,695.27	($9,901.80)
Mountain Bikes	Mountain-100 Black, 48	$1,041,901.60	($19,133.17)
Touring Bikes	Touring-1000 Yellow, 46	$1,016,312.83	($218,141.44)
Road Bikes	Road-650 Black, 52	$973,173.33	($34,113.78)
Road Bikes	Road-650 Red, 60	$970,255.43	($33,138.03)
Road Bikes	Road-550-W Yellow, 48	$950,134.77	($37,330.09)

Figure 125: Sorting a column

We can also represent KPI data, which is a common requirement for dashboard reporting.

Product_Category	Product_Subcategory	Product	Margin	Margin Status
Accessories	Bike Racks	Hitch Rack - 4-Bike	55.25 %	◎
Accessories	Bottles and Cages	Water Bottle - 30 oz.	55.82 %	◎
Accessories	Cleaners	Bike Wash - Dissolver	56.07 %	◎
Accessories	Helmets	Sport-100 Helmet, Black	49.38 %	◎
Accessories	Helmets	Sport-100 Helmet, Blue	49.00 %	◎
Accessories	Helmets	Sport-100 Helmet, Red	49.33 %	◎
Accessories	Hydration Packs	Hydration Pack - 70 oz.	57.09 %	◎
Accessories	Locks	Cable Lock	44.88 %	◎
Accessories	Pumps	Minipump	45.04 %	◎
Accessories	Tires and Tubes	Patch Kit/8 Patches	60.27 %	◎
Bikes	Mountain Bikes	Mountain-100 Black, 38	-2.24 %	●
Bikes	Mountain Bikes	Mountain-100 Black, 42	-1.35 %	●
Bikes	Mountain Bikes	Mountain-100 Black, 44	-0.82 %	●
Bikes	Mountain Bikes	Mountain-100 Black, 48	-1.80 %	●
Bikes	Mountain Bikes	Mountain-100 Silver, 38	-1.97 %	●
Bikes	Mountain Bikes	Mountain-100 Silver, 42	-0.94 %	●
Bikes	Mountain Bikes	Mountain-100 Silver, 44	-0.46 %	●
Bikes	Mountain Bikes	Mountain-100 Silver, 48	0.05 %	●
Bikes	Mountain Bikes	Mountain-200 Black, 38	10.00 %	●
Bikes	Mountain Bikes	Mountain-200 Black, 42	10.07 %	●
Bikes	Mountain Bikes	Mountain-200 Black, 46	10.34 %	●

Figure 126: KPIs in a Power View table report

Visualizing data using matrix in Power View

Matrix visualization is another popular visualization method for analyzing measures across multiple dimensions using row grouping and column grouping. To use it, we begin by selecting all the data fields we would like to visualize in the matrix from the field list.

Figure 127: Selecting data to visualize

As we learned earlier, selecting data from the field list creates a tabular report by default. To switch to matrix visualization, select the table, open the **Design** tab in the ribbon, click **Table**, and select **Matrix**.

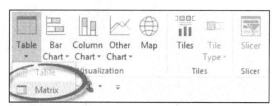

Figure 128: Matrix visualization option

Switching to the matrix visualization puts the measures in the Values area of the field list, and all the dimension columns in the Rows area. We now move CalendarYear to the Columns area to form a matrix report, as shown in the following figure.

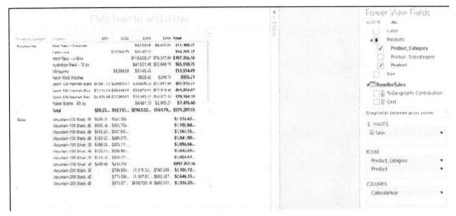

Figure 129: Matrix report in Power View

By default, Power View summarizes measures across the rows and columns to calculate the row totals and column totals, which are represented in bold, as shown in the previous figure. We can turn off the row total, column totals, or both using the Design tab and Totals tab as described previously.

If we need to enable drill-down in the row hierarchy to initially hide the child levels, we can click the **Show Levels** button in the **Design** tab and select **Rows – Enable Drill Down One Level at a Time** as shown in the following figure.

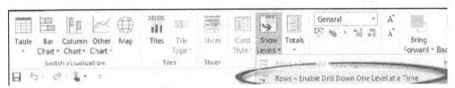

Figure 130: Hiding child levels initially

This will create a drill-down report which is initially collapsed, hiding all the child levels of the hierarchy. In our matrix report, initially we only see the Product Category at the row level. When we click on the Accessories value, we see a drill-down arrow, as shown in the following figure. When we click on the arrow, the data is drilled to the child level, the Product level in our case, with a drill-up arrow to allow us to drill back up to the parent level.

Drill down

Product_Category	2001	2002	2003	2004	Total
Accessories	$20,235.36	$92,735.35	$296,532.88	$161,794.33	$571,297.93
Bikes	$7,395,348.63	$19,056,014.67	$25,551,775.07	$13,300,243.18	$66,302,381.56
Clothing	$343,70.54	$485,587.15	$5/1,804.19	$480,073.16	$1,777,840.84
Components					
Total					

Drill up

Product	2001	2002	2003	2004
Bike Wash - Dissolver			$6,733.09	$4,455.23
Cable Lock		$10,084.70	$6,140.52	
Hitch Rack - 4-Bike			$118,420.47	$79,307.69
Hydration Pack - 70 oz			$41,531.96	$23,986.79
Minipump		$0,369.26	$5,145.43	
Patch Kit/8 Patches			$628.42	$296.78
Sport-100 Helmet, Black	$8,681.73	$24,365.51	$38,406.23	$17,961.00
Sport-100 Helmet, Blue	$7,114.14	$26,440.25	$39,674.01	$17,818.45
Sport-100 Helmet, Red	$8,439.40	$22,960.63	$35,363.41	$14,972.15
Water Bottle - 30 oz			$4,481.33	$2,995.27
Total	$20,235.36	$92,735.35	$296,532.88	$161,794.33

Figure 131: Drill-down and drill-up options

Visualizing data with cards in Power View

Card visualization is a unique and innovative visualization useful for visualizing related data, attributes, or properties of an entity. For example, employee name, age, gender, and marital status fields can be represented together in a card. Similarly, product name, weight, size, color, and photo can be visualized in card format, which can appear as a catalog in the report.

To use the card visualization, we first select all the fields from the field list we would like to see in the card view.

Figure 132: Field list

Next, we open the **Design** tab on the ribbon, click the **Table** item, and select **Card**.

Figure 133: Selecting the card visualization

In the card visualization, the data is represented as shown in the following figure:

Figure 134: Card visualization

If we need to call out these fields in the report, we can switch the card style to callout mode by clicking on the **Card Style** button in the **Design** tab and selecting **Callout** as shown in the following figure.

Figure 135: Changing the card style to callout mode

Figure 136: Card visualization with callout mode enabled

Visualizing data using charts in Power View

Power View provides a rich set of chart visualization tools ranging from column charts and bar charts to scatter charts. Different charts are useful for analysis and comparison of data across different dimensions. In this section we will explore the various chart visualization methods available.

To start, we select all the fields we need to visualize from the field list as shown in the following figure.

Figure 137: Selecting fields to chart

We switch to a **Stacked Column** chart in the **Design** tab in as shown in the following figure.

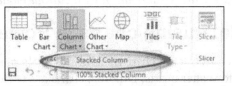

Figure 138: Selecting a stacked column chart

We drag the **Year**, **Quarter**, and **Month** fields into the **AXIS** box and set the **LEGEND** option to **Country** as shown in the following figure.

The resulting graph is shown in Figure 140.

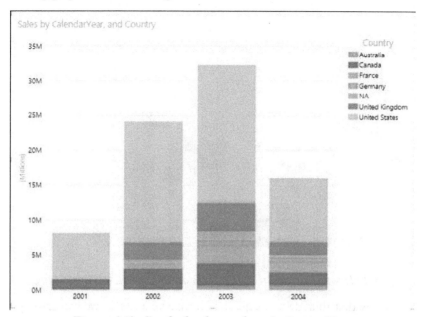

Figure 140: Stacked column chart in Power View

In the horizontal axis, we have a hierarchy of Year, Quarter, and Month; however, by default we can only visualize the parent level. In order to drill down to the quarter level, we need to double-click on a column bar. When we double-click on the 2003 column bar, we see the following graph.

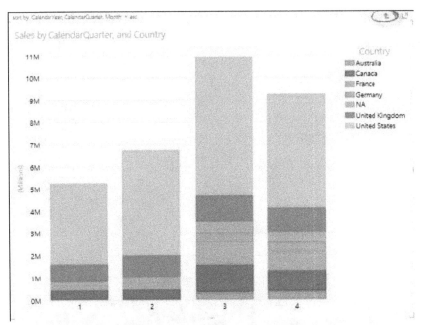

Sales by CalendarQuarter, and Country

Country
Australia
Canaca
France
Germany
NA
United Kingdom
United States

Figure 141: Drilling down in the 2003 column (drill-up arrow circled)

The data is now distributed across quarters for the year 2003. We can drill up by clicking the arrow circled in the previous figure. We can further drill down to the month level by double-clicking on a quarter's column bar.

In this representation of data, we can compare sales across members in the same level of the hierarchy. For example, we can use column charts to make a comparison across years or quarter levels in a given year, but we cannot compare quarters from different years.

If we need to compare the sales across quarters of different years, we can move the **Calendar Year** to the **Horizontal Multiples** section as shown in the following figure.

Figure 142: Reorganizing the column chart

The resulting graph is displayed in the following figure.

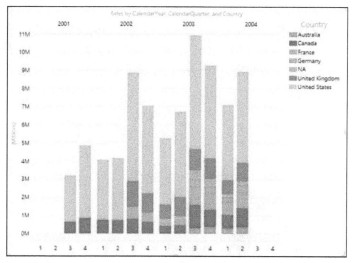

Figure 143: Comparing quarters between years in a column chart

If we need to turn the legends off, change the position of the legend, or turn on data labels, we can do it from the **Layout** tab at the top.

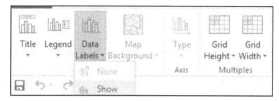

Figure 144: Enabling data labels

If we are not concerned with the absolute sales but want to visualize the contribution of each country to the sales for each quarter, we can switch to a 100% stacked column chart to compare the relative contribution from each country. The resulting graph is:

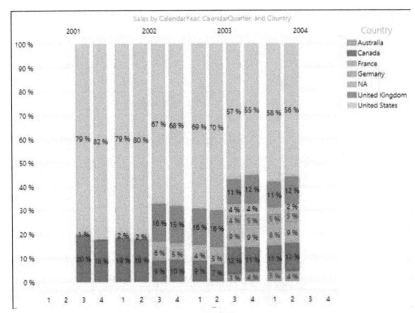

Figure 145: 100% stacked column chart

This chart explains that the rise in sales in 2003 is due to added contribution from certain countries including Germany, Australia, and France to the overall sales.

We can switch to a clustered column chart, which is less compact since it moves the legends to the top to save some horizontal space, but can be useful for relative comparison of absolute sales across each country. To move the legend to the top, click the **Layout** tab, click **Legend**, and select **Show Legend on Top**.

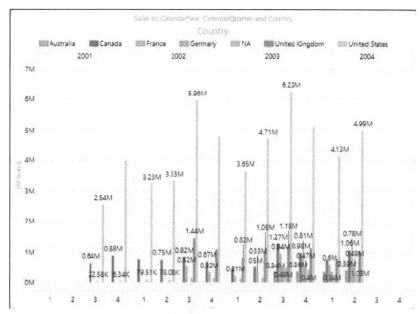

Figure 146: Legend set at top of chart

From the graph in Figure 146, we understand that the sales are observed to be high in Q3 for the United States with the highest sales in Q3 of 2003.

Similar to the column chart, we have horizontal bar charts available, namely the stacked bar chart, 100% stacked bar chart, and clustered bar chart. The same information we charted with the column charts is shown in the following figure as a bar chart.

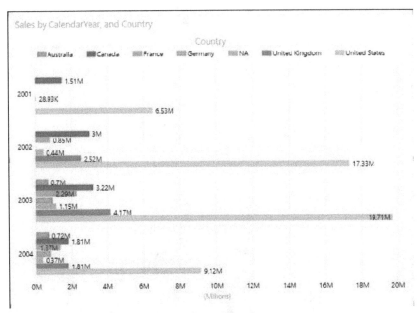

Figure 147: Bar chart

If we observe the same information in bar format, we see that it appears less cluttered than the column format. The bar chart is easier to use for visual comparisons.

Similarly, if we need to study the trend of the sales, cost, and profit values over the months for the various product categories, we can use a line graph with the fields shown in Figure 148.

Figure 148: Selecting fields for a line chart

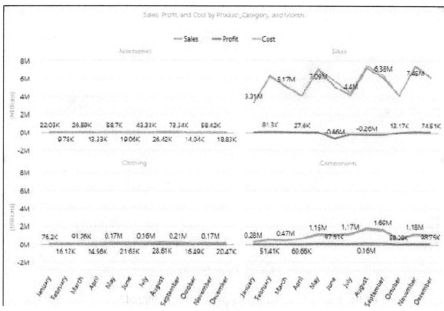

Figure 149: Line chart

This chart shows interesting statistics for bikes; even though the Bikes chart shows good sales from May to August, the cost for bikes is also higher during this period, which explains the loss for this product category. The line graph is popular for similar trend analysis and charting reports.

Pie charts are another graphic tool useful for analyzing the share or contribution of each sector to the total. While designing the data model, we created a calculated measure for % Geography Contribution to measure the contribution of each region to the total sales. This measure can be best represented in a pie chart.

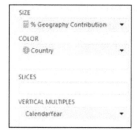

Figure 150: Selecting the measure to chart in a pie chart

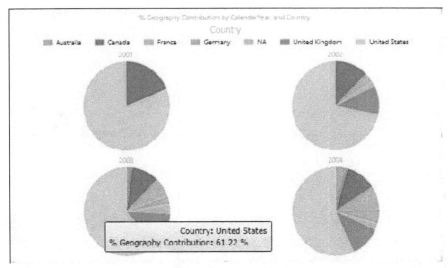

Figure 151: Pie chart

Currently, one of the major limitations of pie charts is their lack of data labels.

One of the most impressive chart visualization tools, the bubble and scatter graph, allows us to measure data simultaneously across multiple dimensions or axes. Consider a scenario where we need to measure the sales, sales target, and profit trend month-on-month from each employee of AdventureWorks in various product categories. Here, we need to slice and dice the Sales, Sales Target, and Profit measures across the Employee, Date, and Product dimensions simultaneously. We can achieve this using the bubble and scatter graph as shown in the following figure.

Σ X VALUE
Sales ▾

Σ Y VALUE
Revised Sales Target ▾

Σ SIZE
Profit ▾

DETAILS
Name ▾

COLOR
Product_Category ▾

PLAY AXIS
Month ▾

| VERTICAL MULTIPLES |

Figure 152: Selecting fields to chart in a bubble and scatter graph

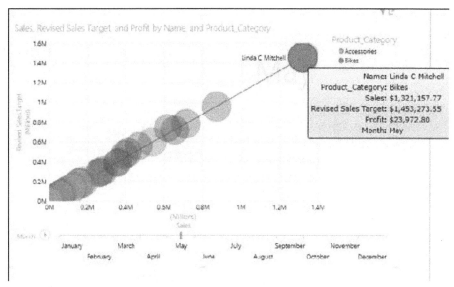

Figure 153: Bubble and scatter graph

In a scatter chart, the x-axis displays one numeric field and the y-axis displays another, making it easy to see the relationship between the two values for all the items in the chart.

In a bubble chart, a third numeric field controls the size of the data points. To view changes in data over time, we add a time field, Month, to scatter and bubble charts with a "play axis."

When we click the play button in the chart, the bubbles travel across the Month axis, growing and shrinking to show how the Profit changes based on the play axis. We can pause at any point to study the data in more detail. When we click a bubble on the chart, we see its history in the trail the bubble has followed over time, as shown in the previous figure.

We added the Product Category field to the Color box for a scatter or bubble chart, which colors the bubbles or scatter points differently according to the different values of the category, overriding the bubble colors.

Visualizing data using maps in Power View reports

Geographical or spatial data can be best visualized using maps in Power View reports. Power View can interpret the Data Category property for each field defined in the tabular model cube, which we discussed in the previous chapter. Fields with data categories like Country, City, and Region are good candidates to be viewed in map form.

Maps in Power View use Bing Maps tiles, so you can zoom and pan as you would with any other Bing map. To make maps work, Power View has to send the data to Bing through a secured web connection for geocoding, so it asks you to enable content. Hence we need to have an Internet connection to visualize maps in Power View.

Consider a scenario where we need to report the % Geography Contribution measure for AdventureWorks across various sales territories for various product categories. We select all the fields desired and switch to the map visualization using the Design tab on the ribbon. We can represent the data as follows:

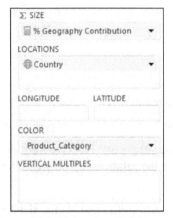

Figure 154: Selecting fields to map

Adding locations and fields places dots on the map. The larger the value, the bigger the dot. When you add a multi-value series, you get pie charts on the map, with the size of the pie chart showing the size of the total as shown in the following figure:

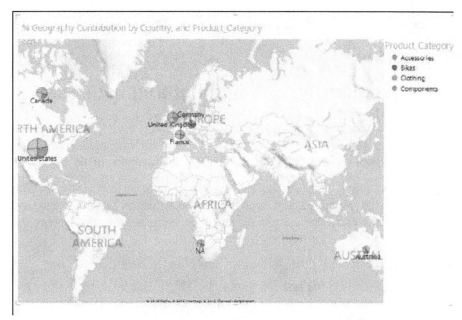

Figure 155: Map visualization

In a map visualization, besides the legend and data label options, we have the option to change the map background in the Layout tab:

Figure 156: Options to change map background

Filtering and slicing in Power View reports

Interactive filtering and highlighting with chart visualization

One of the unique features in Power View is interactive filtering and highlighting with chart visualization, which applies to all other visualizations in the report.

Charts can act as filters, thanks to those relationships in the underlying model. This is interactive filtering, meaning that we can select values directly on a chart and have it filter other data regions in the view. If we select one column in a column chart, this automatically:

- Filters the values in all the tables, tiles, and bubble charts in the report.
- Adds highlighting to bar and column charts. It highlights the parts of other bar and column charts that pertain to that value, showing the contribution of the filtered values to the original values.

We can press and hold Ctrl to select multiple values. To clear the filter, click inside the filter, but not on a value.

Interactive filtering also works with charts with multiple series. Clicking one section of a bar in a bar chart filters to that specific value. Clicking an item in the legend filters all the sections in that series.

Consider the following report in Power View where we display sales by the product category in a column chart, sales by the calendar year in a bar chart, and the percent geography contribution to the sales in a pie chart.

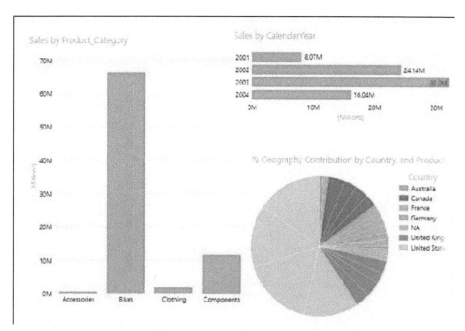

Figure 157: Report with column, bar, and pie charts

Now if we are interested to know sales for the Components category for each year and each country's contribution to sales in the Components category, we can click on the Components bar in the column chart and the report will dynamically slice and filter the other charts to highlight only the sales for the Components category. The result is shown in the following figure.

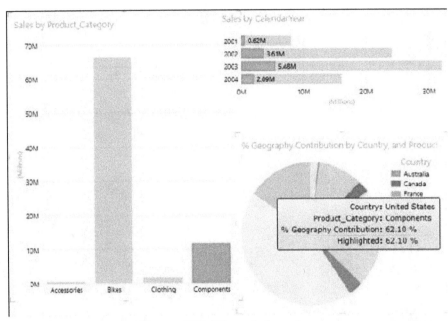

Figure 158: Filtered chart data

This interactive filtering in each visualization, which applies to all the other visualizations in the report, is a very a useful feature for ad hoc analytics and reporting.

Filters

Besides interactive filtering, we can define filters in the Filters area of the Power View report. We can apply filters to individual visualizations in the report or apply them to the entire report. To add the filter, we need to drag and drop the field from the **Field** list to the **Filters** area.

Let us add Product Category as a filter in the Filters area as shown in the following figure.

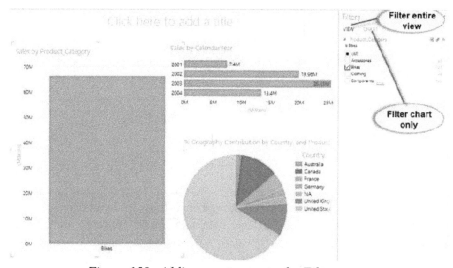

Figure 159: Adding a category to the Filters area

In the Filters area, we have distinct values of fields for each filter listed as shown in Figure 159. By default, all the values are selected in the filter. We can use the check boxes to select the individual Product Category fields that we want to view. If we need to reset the filter, we can click the **Clear Filter** option. To delete the filter, we can click the **Delete Filter** option as shown in the following figure.

Figure 160: Filter options

We also have an Advanced Filter Mode option, which is very useful when we need to filter a field with a large number of unique values and it isn't practical to filter the values by selecting the values individually.

If we click on **Advanced Filter Mode**, the following screen appears.

Figure 161: Advanced filter options

In the Advanced Filter Mode, we can specify multiple filter conditions using the And and Or operators. If the field value satisfies the condition, the data is displayed in the report. The advanced filter options change depending on the data type of the field to be filtered.

If we apply the advanced filter to a field of the text data type, we see the following options.

Figure 162: Text data type filter options

We can search for a value within a visualization-level or view-level filter on a text field, and then choose whether to apply a filter to it. The portion of a field's values that match the search text are highlighted in the search results list. The search is not case-sensitive, so searching for "Bikes" yields the same results as "bikes".

We can also use wildcard characters like the question mark (?) and asterisk (*). A question mark matches any single character; an asterisk matches any sequence of characters. If we want to find an actual question mark or asterisk, we need to type a tilde (~) before the character.

If we search for fields with a date data type, we see the following options.

Figure 163: Date data type filter options

For fields with a numeric data type, we see the following options.

Figure 164: Numeric data type filter options

Slicers

Slicers are another kind of filter. They filter everything on the page. Power View slicers look very much like slicers in PowerPivot for Excel. We can create a single-column table from any field that is an attribute, and then convert the table into a slicer. Each value is a button, and a button in the top corner clears (resets) the filter. To select a value, just click that button. The data is filtered in the report immediately.

You can select multiple values by holding the **Ctrl** key when you click.

We can also select everything except a certain set of values by resetting the filter with the button in the top corner, and then using **Ctrl** + click to clear specific values. This shows overall values excluding the values not selected.

You can add more than one slicer to your report. Slicers filter each other; for example, if we have two slicers, one for Product Category and one for Products, when we click a category in the former, it filters the latter to show only products in that category. The filtering effects of all slicers are combined.

Unlike chart filters, slicers:

- Filter charts. They do not highlight charts.

- Are saved with the report. When you save, close, and reopen a report, the same values will be selected in the slicer.
- Can use image fields. Behind the scenes, Power View uses the Row Identifier field for that image as the filter in the slicer.

In order to create slicers in the report, we need to select the field from the field list that we want to use as slicer, and click the **Slicer** option in the **Design** tab on the ribbon.

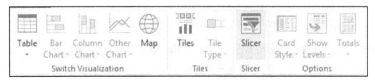

Figure 165: Slicer option on ribbon

Slicers for the Product Category field are displayed in the Power View report as shown in the following figure. When we click on the individual values in the slicers, Accessories in this case, the entire report is filtered for that value.

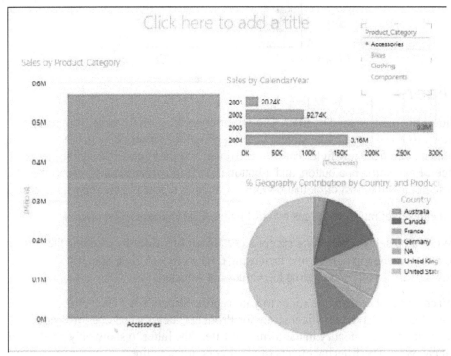

Figure 166: Applying a slicer to a report

Slicers can be useful as filters when we need to filter the entire report using a field that has less distinct values. When the number of unique values in a field are many, we can choose the advanced filter mode in the Filters area.

Of the different ways that we can filter and highlight data in our report, each way behaves differently when you save a report:

- If we set a filter or slicer in design view, the state of the slicer or filter is saved with the report.
- If we highlight a chart in design view, its state is not saved with the report.

Designing a dashboard in Power View

In the previous sections, we learned all the visualizations and filtering options available with Power View and what data can be best represented by each visualization. Bringing them all together, we can create interactive dashboards for end users and analysts that will allow them to make informed decisions better and faster.

In this section, we will design the AdventureWorks sales dashboard to provide an executive-level summary of sales, profit, year-over-year comparisons, and the contribution of each region.

We create the following dashboard using the visualizations we discussed previously.

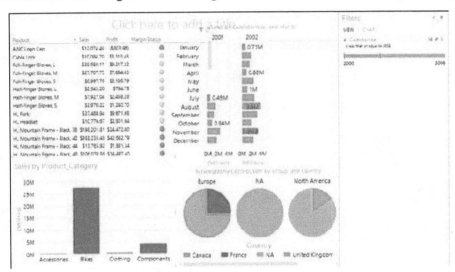

Figure 167: Power View dashboard

In dashboards, it is preferred to represent detail-level data and KPIs in tabular format. Hence we represent product-level details along with the sales, profit, and margin KPI using table visualization.

In order to showcase year-over-year comparisons for product sales, we choose to represent the monthly sales figure with a bar chart with Calendar Year as the horizontal multiple. We could have represented the same chart using a column chart visualization, but due to horizontal space constraints, we choose to represent it with a bar chart (which is also visually better for yearly comparisons).

To represent the regional contribution, we use pie charts as horizontal multiples to represent the percent geography contributions. Pie charts best represent such data.

We choose to represent the sales by Product Category using a column chart, which is useful for interactive filtering and highlighting, specifically for filtering the Product Details table.

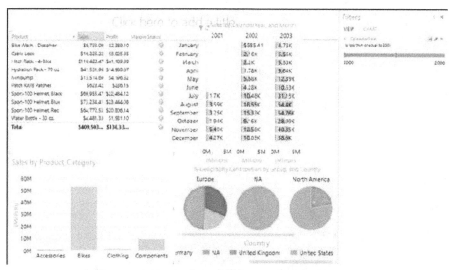

Figure 168: Applying filters to the dashboard

We add a Calendar Year filter in the Filters area, which can help limit the data in the bar chart for yearly comparisons.

Once we have all the visualization and filters in place for the dashboard, we add a title to the report and adjust its position and font using the **Text** tab. The Text tab appears only when the mouse pointer is in the text box.

Figure 169: Text options

Next, we add the AdventureWorks logo image by clicking the **Picture** button in the **Power View** tab on the ribbon:

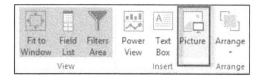

Figure 170: Picture option

We position the logo as shown in the following figure.

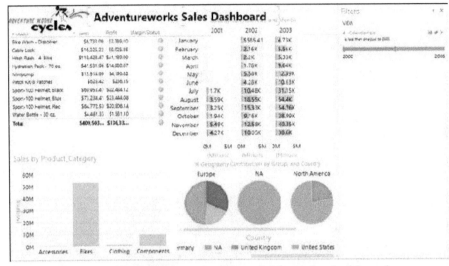

Figure 171: Adding an image and title to the dashboard

Next, we can set an image in the background of the report by clicking the **Set Image** option in the **Power View** tab on the ribbon.

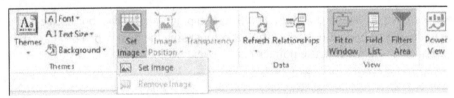

Figure 172: Set Image option

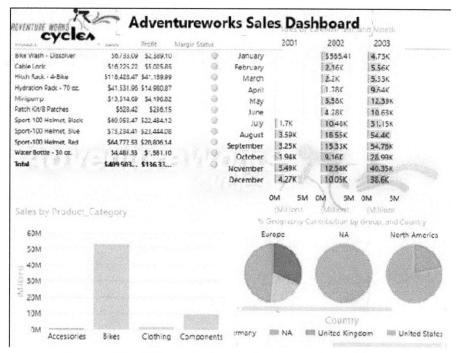

Figure 173: Adding a background image to the dashboard

We can also set the transparency of the image and its position to Fit, Stretch, Tile, or Center in the **Background Image** area in the **Power View** tab.

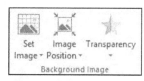

Figure 174: Background Image options

Finally, to make the Power View report visually appealing, we can change the theme and background of the Power View report using the **Themes** options as shown in the following figure.

Figure 175: Themes options in Power View dashboard

The dashboard is now ready for use in reporting and analytics.

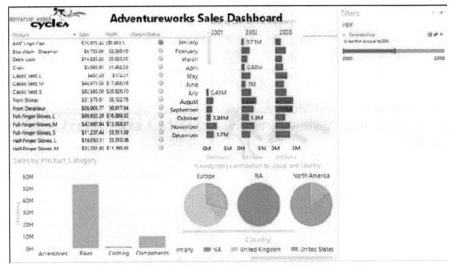

Figure 176: Completed Power View dashboard

Using your creativity and UI expertise, you can create visually appealing and colorful reports for analytics and reporting.

Summary

In summary, Power View is a great reporting and analytics tool with a rich set of visualization options for data exploration and business intelligence.

The new SSAS tabular model provides BI developers the flexibility of easily creating data models with minimum complexity that can be consumed by the Power View report.

Hopefully you will now be excited and curious to explore these and other new products introduced in the Microsoft BI stack.